'I loved *How to Become a Money Magnet*. It's packed with ...
money as well as practical advice on how to unblock the flow of abu...
it I've cleared clutter from every area of my life and continue to attract an...
money-making opportunities. I would recommend anyone who wants more wealth in the...
life to read it.'
Rachel Elnaugh, star of *Dragons' Den* and founder of Red Letter Days

'As soon as I finished reading *How to Become a Money Magnet* I was immediately inundated
with offers of work, positive replies to film proposals I'd sent months before and emails
from people wanting to collaborate on incredible projects. Something has shifted in me
exactly as if an electromagnet has been switched on – I'm attracting well-paid work, but
even more importantly, it's work that I care about with people I love. I recommend this to
anyone who thinks money is hard to come by.'
Andy Lee, documentary film maker

'I'm sure this book *How to become a Money Magnet* will help lots of people and they will pick
up its underlying message. It is brilliant that you have written it.'
Diana Cooper

'This book is full of inspiring real-world examples. It doesn't matter who you are or where
you're coming from, you too can become a Money Magnet.'
Chantal Cooke, of Passion for the Planet

'Initially skeptical, when I read *How to Become a Money Magnet* I was completely
transformed. Beliefs going back to childhood were uncovered. It was enlightening.
I am now a Money Magnet!'
Sally Inkster, of Diva Dressing

'If you want to "boost" your life to greater heights and attract more money in the process,
Marie-Claire is a powerhouse of positive energy that you must have on your team. I do!'
Paul Avins, the Turbo Business Coach

'I have just finished my ceremony for eliminating my old beliefs on money and wealth. I
wrote out my old beliefs on strips of paper and ceremonially burned them whilst loudly
exclaiming that they were wrong, I was wrong and that I no longer held to such beliefs
because I now have new, better, more abundant ones!! The neighbours may think I have
gone mad, but it felt great. Thanks again for helping me find myself.'
Phil Birch, business editor and director, the3rdi.co.uk

'I know since I've read *How to Become a Money Magnet* that my attitude towards money has
changed and I'm welcoming it with open arms now because I deserve it. It now comes to
me easily and naturally.'
Amanda Daniels, of Koogar

'I have now started to read *How to Become a Money Magnet*. The book is more down to earth
than *The Secret* and far easier to relate to.'
David Crayton, of Crayton Marketing

'*How to Become a Money Magnet* is a breath of fresh air. The anecdotes and Marie-Claire's own candour about her relationship with money makes this a must read for anyone who wants to improve their financial situation. This book comes straight from the heart, is extremely well-written, and offers lots of practical tips. Thoroughly recommended.'
Hazel Thomson, director, Coach2Deliver

'While many people only look at the "physical" reality of money, I've been researching the mechanics of money creation and beyond. Marie-Claire does a wonderful job of exploring the metaphysics of money in her book so that you too can harness the energy and have it flow to you. You WILL find this book valuable!'
Bobby Gill

'*How to Become a Money Magnet* is EXCELLENT – I advise anyone out there to go and buy a copy for themselves or at least a copy for someone you love.'
Maurice Kellegher, of Motivational Networking

'Any woman who writes a book on attracting wealth gets my vote – a great read!'
Jane Kenyon, of Well Heeled Divas

'I was SO meant to read your book… at the perfect time… I had been advertising my dog walking service through leaflet drops, newspaper advertising, leaving my cards with vets and pet stores – and wasn't getting any leads… However when I started reading your book last Thursday, I got a call that evening from my first client, and received another on Sunday from a client wanting me to look after her dog for three weeks, which would net me $1000! Thank you, thank you, thank you!'
Sue Dingwall, director, Positive Puppies

'I bought *How to Become a Money Magnet* on Wednesday… had a meeting with a prospect who has subsequently offered me some work; had another successful meeting with another company that is very likely to provide me with work in the future; received the *4Front Chamber of Commerce* magazine containing my short article and picture… and I've only read the first chapter!!!! So I've decided to send a copy to my sister for her birthday.'
Anna Cutts, of Redstart Consulting

'What an inspiration – Marie-Claire has caught the negativity of the "credit crunch" and turned it around to make it work positively for me – and for many others I'm sure. This book will be one I will keep to refresh me when I need reminding, and also to recommend to anyone experiencing money troubles or a change in their career. I can wholeheartedly recommend this book as my book of the year!'
Jo Pemberton

'This book really works, so order a copy… start doing the exercises in the book, of course at your own pace, and with a bit of angel energy, expect MIRACLES! I can thoroughly recommend Marie-Claire and her book. Change your thoughts today and make big changes to your life!'
Jane

'I haven't even finished the book yet (nearly there, last inch to go) and miracles are already happening. Thank you, Marie-Claire… you are like a female Harry Potter.'
Susie, Sussex

How to Become a
MONEY
Magnet

How to Become a
MONEY
Magnet

Marie-Claire Carlyle

HAY HOUSE

Australia • Canada • Hong Kong • India
South Africa • United Kingdom • United States

First published and distributed in the United Kingdom by:
Hay House UK Ltd, 292B Kensal Rd, London W10 5BE. Tel.: (44) 20 8962 1230;
Fax: (44) 20 8962 1239. www.hayhouse.co.uk

Published and distributed in the United States of America by:
Hay House, Inc., PO Box 5100, Carlsbad, CA 92018-5100. Tel.: (1) 760 431 7695 or
(800) 654 5126; Fax: (1) 760 431 6948 or (800) 650 5115. www.hayhouse.com

Published and distributed in Australia by:
Hay House Australia Ltd, 18/36 Ralph St, Alexandria NSW 2015.
Tel.: (61) 2 9669 4299; Fax: (61) 2 9669 4144. www.hayhouse.com.au

Published and distributed in the Republic of South Africa by:
Hay House SA (Pty), Ltd, PO Box 990, Witkoppen 2068.
Tel./Fax: (27) 11 467 8904. www.hayhouse.co.za

Published and distributed in India by:
Hay House Publishers India, Muskaan Complex, Plot No.3, B-2, Vasant Kunj,
New Delhi – 110 070. Tel.: (91) 11 4176 1620; Fax: (91) 11 4176 1630.
www.hayhouse.co.in

Distributed in Canada by:
Raincoast, 9050 Shaughnessy St, Vancouver, BC V6P 6E5. Tel.: (1) 604 323 7100;
Fax: (1) 604 323 2600

A catalogue record for this book is available from the British Library.

Previously published by Miracle Club in 2009, ISBN 978-0-9561563-0-3.

ISBN 978-1-84850-238-3

Printed and bound in Great Britain by
TJ International, Padstow, Cornwall

Mixed Sources
Product group from well-managed
forests and other controlled sources
www.fsc.org Cert no. SGS-COC-2482
© 1996 Forest Stewardship Council

In memory of
Humphrey Broad-Davies

About the Author

Marie-Claire has spent most of her working life coaching others to fulfil their true potential. As sales manager and later as sales director, Marie-Claire used her skills and knowledge to ensure that her team consistently overachieved sales targets. As a professional coach and Feng Shui consultant, Marie-Claire helps her clients to clear out the clutter that hides their true magnificence and wealth (www.marieclairecarlyle.com).

Having discovered the way to wealth herself, Marie-Claire developed the 'How to Become a Money Magnet' one-day workshop. The results were consistently positive and she was asked to capture the essence of the workshop in a book (www.howtobecomeamoneymagnet.com).

Marie-Claire runs her own coaching and consultancy business, helping both companies and individuals to achieve their true potential, in every sense of the word. As well as writing several books, Marie-Claire has also founded Miracle Club which provides affordable group coaching to inspire everyone to fulfil their true potential for happiness (www.miracleclub.com).

Marie-Claire holds two business degrees, and is a qualified life coach (DipLCH), and NLP practitioner and an accredited Feng Shui consultant (FSSA) and Space Clearer. Marie-Claire has also studied at the College of Psychic Studies, The School of Insight and Intuition and extensively with Diana Cooper, where she qualified as a Transform Your Life teacher. She has taught at local colleges, where her subjects have included life coaching, cosmic ordering and Feng Shui, and she now facilitates workshops and events across the world.

Acknowledgements

Thank you to:

The many friends and students who have attended my classes and the 'How to Become a Money Magnet!' workshops. You've inspired me in so many ways, including in the writing of this book. Thank you for your stories.

My mother, Ann Broad-Davies, who really demonstrates the power of love every day. Her support and faith in me are unflinching and I thank her from the bottom of my heart for making my world so beautiful.

My friends, who have stood by my side at each turning of the road. Thank you for loving all the aspects of me and not just the 'pretty' ones.

Bob Proctor and his guests on the 2008 Caribbean cruise, all of whom helped me glimpse what was possible, and especially Mitch Mortimer, who believed in me.

Contents

Foreword

This book really made me think about my money habits. Considering that money makes the world go round, it's surprising how little we understand it or know about it. This book challenges you at every turn, with techniques that can change your money mindset in miraculous time. It's a brilliant book that will really make you think about where you have been going wrong with money all this time, and how easy it is to fix. It made me realise that I hadn't treated money very well in the past. I thought I loved it and the things that I could do with it, but I wasn't dedicating enough time to it. This book really made me see that if I wanted more money in my life, then I had to think about it in a fundamentally different way. Now I treat money like the precious commodity it is. Every time I fill the car with fuel, for instance, I think of the money paying for it as pure gold dust that gets me where I want to be.

Money had caused me a lot of pain in the past, because it would come and go so quickly. I had to refocus and change that pain into pleasure. Money was a dirty word, and I got rid of it like it was a bad smell. As I cried over my debts it looked impossible to turn them around. With the help of this book, though, I managed to get a grip on my debts, and envision a life where my finances blossom. And you can, too.

Marie-Claire made me think about my approach to money. I used to think that if I wanted more money, the only way to get it was to work harder, because that's what I had always done as a teenager. I always had two or three jobs to fund my love of clothes. As a business owner I know that there are only a certain amount of hours in the day. Yet by learning from Marie-Claire, I've realised that, in fact, by changing my attitude, I can actually work less and accomplish more.

Now my first response to the money I have is to ask 'How can I keep hold of it?' not 'How can I spend it?' – and it comes in all the more freely now because, once I have it, it stays put!

What I've enjoyed most about *How to Become a Money Magnet!* is that it is easy to read and follow. Most of the exercises I did in my little notepad while sitting in a coffee shop.

Since reading the book, I have been analysing the messages about money that I'd picked up over the years. 'Money is the root of all evil' was my favourite. I have learned to challenge this by, first, reminding myself of my personal 'bigger picture': I have many charitable ambitions and want to make a difference for women, particularly around childbirth. I've realised that the more money I have, the more of a difference I can make. Money is not, therefore, the root of all evil; it is actually a route to all good. That is what this book will teach you: making money for its own sake won't bring you fulfilment, but making money so you can do good with it, well that's a win/win scenario.

This book has taught me how to let go of the power that money had over me, and it has been brilliant watching everything turn around right in front of my eyes. Money doesn't control me any more – I control it, measure it, love it and monitor it, but most importantly, spend time magnetising it. Most of all, it's just a load of fun. Have fun as you – and your finances – flourish!

Jo Cameron, BEng, MA, Chartered MCIPD

Co-Founder and Director – Women on Their Way Ltd
The global leaders in women's events and conferences
– 'Global Connectors of Women'
Professional speaker, author of *Flourish* (due out in 2010) and BBC contributor (formerly of BBC's *The Apprentice*), Patron of SANDS – the Stillbirth and Neonatal Death Charity

Introduction

Thank you for choosing this book. Congratulations, too, on acknowledging your desire for more money and your intention to change your reality.

In an era when the 'greedy' are receiving their comeuppance and when doing things 'just for the money' is no longer acceptable, it is easy to believe that money is a dirty word. When we believe that money is a dirty word, we shy away from it and, in so doing, we turn our backs on our full potential.

This book is about how money is simply a reflection of our value, both our self-value and the value that we are providing to others.

The book is in three parts: Part 1 takes a look at the theory and at your current situation. Parts 2 and 3 provide a two-stage route to becoming a Money Magnet. Stage one explains how to attract some money immediately (after all, most of us don't want an extended plan of action – we want it now!). Stage two shows how to create and maintain your long-term, sustainable Money Magnet status.

The 'How to Become a Money Magnet!' Workshop

There have been lots of books about how to get rich and how to use the 'law of attraction' to get what you want in life, and yet there were still plenty of people who wanted to come on the 'How to Become a Money Magnet!' workshops.

These one-day workshops were held once a month in a beautiful location in the UK. Following the workshop, people immediately started to attract more money into their lives, and my postbox was filled with delighted thank you notes. Whatever we were doing, it was working!

One of my favourites was the story of a woman called Geraldine:

■ Case study: It Starts with a Decision

I would describe Geraldine as one of life's 'hard workers'. Now a grandmother, she was still working six days a week at minimum wage, and what she did earn she normally gave away to others. When I first met Geraldine, I was struck by her lack of self-confidence. Her head was held low and she looked like she had the world on her shoulders. She was a kind and friendly woman. She was always thinking of the others in the group, and I had the impression that she didn't care for herself as much as she cared for others – that is, until she decided that she wanted to be a Money Magnet!

It always starts with a decision. A simple decision signals a readiness to shift from the status quo. Your decision was to read this book. Geraldine's decision was to invest her hard-earned cash on the 'How to Become a Money Magnet!' workshop.

Within three months of the workshop, Geraldine's world had changed. She started to attract money in ways that she could never have imagined.

At one point, her employers corrected an error in her pay, resulting in three years' back pay!

She managed to move into a new house and to buy herself a car.

The last time I saw Geraldine, she looked 15 years younger: her face was lit up with a huge smile and, wherever she went, she seemed to attract lovely people and children to her side.

Congratulations, Geraldine, for choosing to become a Money Magnet!

How Was the 'How to Become a Money Magnet!' Workshop Conceived?

The original 'How to Become a Money Magnet!' workshop developed out of a combination of factors:

1. I trained as a 'Transform Your Life' teacher with Diana Cooper's School of Transformation. In fact, Diana Cooper was probably the first person who introduced me to the Law of Attraction, long before we'd heard of the film *The Secret* or Barbel Mohr's book, *Cosmic Ordering*. Diana has now published more than 18 books, including *A Little Light on the Spiritual Laws* and *Transform Your Life*.

2. I trained as a Feng Shui consultant with the Feng Shui Academy. Feng Shui looks at how we can change energy through the use of ritual and

intention. These elements became pivotal parts of the workshop.

3. My financial success as a sales manager and, later, as a sales director for a software company was great experience. For example, I know what ingredients are required to take a young graduate to a six-figure salary in his or her first year of work.

4. My personal experience of both the lows of debt and the highs of huge income contributed to my 'knowledge bank'. What I learned about the common factors in moving from one of these states to the other was a vital source of information.

From Famine to Feast to Famine to Feast ...

My career has taken me from retail sales to sales management in FMCG (Fast-Moving Consumer Goods, in case you're not familiar with the term!), and from fashion sales management to photocopier and software sales management. I've suffered the lows of being a very average salesperson and the highs of being an exceptionally good sales manager. My income has gone up and down along the way. Times of feast bring back memories of luxury travel abroad, penthouse apartments and flashy sports cars. Times of famine meant mounting credit card debt and living in someone else's home.

Looking back, I only ever actually focused on money when I went into debt. Debt became my wake-up call. Earning money was the relatively easy part of the equation: I would find a job that I really wanted to do and that stretched me a little; I'd prepare well for the interview and then I would expect to get the job. It always worked. I realise now that it was the motivation of needing more money that pushed me to decide to do something different about my circumstances.

However, once in a job I would lose interest in the money I was earning. I no longer had any respect for it. I was happy to spend it, mind. It was the spending of it that upset the balance, in more ways than one. I knew how to fill the bucket, but I was emptying it as fast as I was filling it. When it was so empty that I was digging a hole in its bottom, I would wake up again and realise that I had to do something different to attract more money.

This cycle reflected how much I valued myself. Money was a useful guide. I realised that I had to make money my friend. More important, I had to make myself my own friend. The higher my level of self-worth, the more I would be valued by others and the more money I would attract. When I became bored or unhappy in a job, I was no longer valuing myself by staying in that job. If I didn't leave the job (ironically, because of the money!), I would (unconsciously) find a way to lose the money. I would then have to change jobs in order to attract more money. Talk about self-sabotage!

In the end, this pattern wasn't sustainable. In 2003 I left my job as sales director of a software company and I spent a couple of years retraining and getting to know myself as a person I could love and respect. I now work for myself, doing what I really want to do and pushing myself to achieve my dreams. I have taken responsibility for how much money I now earn and for how much I value myself, and I keep an eye on the meter! This book shares with you all that I have learned on the way to becoming – and staying – a Money Magnet!

What Prompted Me to Write This Book?

After I'd been running the 'How to Become a Money Magnet!' workshops for a year, I was invited to record an interview on the subject with Chantal Cooke of Passion for the Planet radio. (You will read more about Chantal later, as she also worked with me to uncover her true magnificence and the essence within her that makes her a Money Magnet.) Our interview was recorded onto a CD entitled 'How to Be a Money Magnet!' The CD was subsequently bought by iTunes and is now available across the world as a download at www.audible.com.

Some months ago I received a heart-warming letter from a lawyer in London who had bought my CD. Through a number of circumstances, this woman had lost her home and was now living in a hostel, yet she had not yet given up hope. She enclosed a postal order for £20 for the CD and told me that she'd already listened to it 30 times. Her story, as well as many other such heartfelt stories, inspired me to write this book, so that others might regain a sense of hope and be able to turn their lives around.

We are currently living in a time when you can't turn on the news without hearing another sad tale of the 'credit crunch'. Most of us know someone, if not ourselves, who has been made redundant or has been asked to work fewer hours. Our high streets are littered with closed-down shops and businesses. Our savings have diminished in value and lines of credit have simply dried up. And it seems that every time we listen to the news or pick up a paper, there is always someone blaming someone else for the 'mess' we are all in.

We blame the banks, the greedy City traders or the Government. And while we are pointing the finger at others, we are distracted from looking within. While we are using our energy to cast blame on others, we have less energy for ourselves. If you keep your focus on bad news, you will attract bad news. Shift your focus and keep a lookout for the good news – the companies who are thriving and adding to their staff, or the people you know who have found what they love to do and have turned it into a successful business, maybe even financed by a redundancy payment.

The good news is out there if you decide to see it, I promise you. Only the other day I was chatting with a journalist from our local paper and she told me how they were putting together a news item on all the new businesses that had recently rented premises in our city. That's what I call a good news story! When we all start shifting our focus, the media will then follow suit and we'll have the ingredients for turning the corner of any recession. When we stop blaming others and choose instead to take responsibility for our own status, then we can start to become Money Magnets, irrespective of external circumstances.

Are you taking in all the negativity or have you found a way to stay positive amid the gloom?

The Secret is a small documentary film produced by Rhonda Byrne that has sold millions of copies on DVD in the United States. The film was successful enough to be featured on both the Oprah Winfrey and Larry King shows, and is now a top seller on Amazon. It is a wonderful introduction to how we are responsible for the quality of our lives and how we have the influence to have more of what we want – and less of what we don't want. It has a very positive message and as such is the perfect antedote to the negativity in our newspapers.

Bob Proctor is the star of *The Secret*. He has been educating people on how to be rich for more than 40 years. When Bob was in London not so long ago, I attended his seminar. It can be challenging sometimes to be positive when everyone around you is talking of a 'credit crunch'. However, while there, I heard something that helped me put the words 'credit crunch' into a better perspective.

A young couple, Hannah and Joe, attended the whole three-day seminar and shared this story with us: on hearing people talk of a 'credit crunch', Hannah, who rarely watched TV, turned to Joe one morning and asked, 'Darling, I've been hearing a lot about the credit crunch. Is that a new cereal?' Now every time I hear the words 'credit crunch' I feel an inner smile instead of the usual sigh.

Has it ever occurred to you that the credit crunch is a 'heaven sent' way for us to clear out our clutter and get focused on what we really want to be doing? I am passionate about helping people clear the clutter that gets in the way of their true potential. Clutter, whether it's in our homes, our bodies, our lives or in our thoughts, clouds us from our purpose and clarity. Remember the lightness you felt when you last cleared some clutter in your home, office or car? If you have ever done a detox programme, you will know how much clearer your thoughts become. Clutter is a distraction from our true essence.

In the same way, our society has been focused on material gain without always balancing it with value given. Employees have demanded more and more money and benefits, irrespective of a company's financial position. We have spent money that we didn't have. We have bought houses when we had no money in the bank. We buy the sofa because we don't need to pay for it for 12 months. We use the credit card and worry about it later. We have forgotten how to value money.

Nature is all about balance. When we tip the scales too much one way, nature demands that we bring ourselves back to balance. In many ways, the recessions that we experience are a chance to clear out our clutter and to get back to what is really important.

Clutter Hides Us from Our Truth

More than one client has complained to me that her business has struggled because of a recession. Sally ran an events company, hosting fun days out for women. Over the previous several months, the phone had stopped ringing with enquiries and her bookings diary had been full of blank pages. 'Marie-Claire' she said. 'My business is really suffering because of the changing economy. What can I do?'

This 'What can I do?' was a rhetorical question, implying that there was nothing she *could* do. She was a victim of circumstance. And so I asked Sally a direct question to get to the truth of the situation: 'What's the real reason you are attracting fewer clients?' Quick as a flash and clearly caught off-guard, she said 'It's because my heart's just not in it any more.'

Once we deal with the truth, it becomes easier to improve the situation. Once Sally recognised that her heart was no longer in hosting women's events, it was easier for her to move on to what does make her happy: Sally's true skill and passion lies in helping women to dress in a way that flatters their natural assets. Recognising this, Sally launched her new company, Diva Dressing (www.divadressing.co.uk) to advise women on their wardrobes.

Shortly afterwards, Sally went on to host a hugely successful women's fundraising event. Combining her event-management skills with her expertise as a personal stylist, Sally hosted a Red Carpet Diva Dressing Swop Shop evening that significantly raised the profile of her new company. This in turn led to greater revenues and profits.

The alternative would have been for Sally to stay blaming 'the recession' for the downfall in her business. So don't blame 'recession', 'the credit crunch' or 'the economic downturn' for your situation, no matter how tempting this may be. The economic climate is too convenient an excuse for you to do nothing. Instead, use it as a way to clear out your clutter.

When we blame external circumstances or even other people for our situation, we place ourselves in the role of 'victim'. This book is to remind you that you are not a victim. You are the director of your own life. You have the power to change your world. If you wish to attract more money into your life, then this book will help you do just that, recession or no recession!

This book is not about how to run a business or how to do your accounts more efficiently. This book takes a look at WHY you are attracting a certain amount of money into your life and how you can 'tweak the magnet' to attract more money into your life. It is based on the 'How to Become a Money Magnet!' workshop, which has delivered results time and time again.

'I just wanted to say thank you for a great Money Magnet workshop. I thoroughly enjoyed the day and have the following to report:

'The next day my husband informed me that his business was now going to give me a small salary, and the weekend following the workshop I put out a request for a new client. Almost immediately the phone rang. It was someone who had just moved into the area wanting to negotiate a weekly massage for an hour and a half each time! I am sure you have received many other similar messages. Most days I remind myself that I am abundant – thank you once again!'

– Rosie, holistic therapist and part-time company secretary, Sussex, UK

There Are No Real Coincidences in Life

You have found this book because you have no doubt reached a point where 'enough is enough!' You are ready to take full responsibility for the amount of money you attract. You recognise a true desire for more money in your bank account and you are ready to do something different in order to change your financial circumstances, NOW!

Congratulations on taking the first step in taking the time to read this book. In doing so, you are sending the first clear sign to your subconscious that you are ready for significant change in your life. You are ready to welcome in wealth. You are ready to be truly happy.

If you have already read some books on money management, abundance or the Law of Attraction, and nothing has changed in your financial status, don't worry. Relax.

Everyone has a turning point, a 'breakthrough moment', and having watched so many people find it on the 'How to Become a Money Magnet!' workshops, I have every reason to anticipate a shift in your fortunes as a result of this book. Mind you, the book does work best when you follow my suggestions!

Just Read the Book!

'I had been advertising my dog-walking services through leaflet drops, newspaper advertising, leaving my cards with vets and pet stores and wasn't getting any leads … However, when I started reading your book last Thursday I got a call from my first client, and received another call on Sunday from a client wanting me to look after her dog for three weeks – which would net me $1,000!'

– Sue Dingwall, Positive Puppies, Sydney

How to Read This Book

This book has been written in an ordered sequence. Part 1 takes you through the theory of how to become a Money Magnet, and takes a look at your current circumstances. Part 2 looks at how you can start to attract more money into your life immediately by following some basic steps. Part 3 lays the foundation required for becoming a lifelong Money Magnet.

It's best to read the book in the order it was written. You will receive maximum benefit if you make time to do the exercises as they arise in the book. The original 'How to Become a Money Magnet!' workshop worked because the participants did all the exercises.

At the end of each chapter is a checklist. The questions there serve as a prompt to your natural intuition. You have all the answers for you. Allow these questions to bring out the truths that you need to access to become a Money Magnet.

Throughout the book you will discover some repetition. This is intended. It is part of the process of transforming you into a Money Magnet!

Congratulations again on reading this book. It's the first step in taking responsibility for the amount of money you attract into your life.

'The "How to Become a Money Magnet!" workshop has enabled me to sort out the money in my life.'

– *Dr Sandy Clyne, who went on to write and publish the book* Organise Your Home Office

---

Quick Check: Are You a 'Poor Me' OR a 'Lucky Me'?

- Is your glass half-full or half-empty?

- Are you saving for a rainy day or for an unexpected holiday?

- Do you love your job or is it just a way to pay the bills?

- Is your financial situation all the fault of someone else or are you proud of what you have achieved?

- Do you hold regrets or are you happy for the learning experiences?

- Is it 'all their fault' or were you steering your own ship?

- Is it all down to the recession or to your own personal choices?

- Are you destined to continue as you are or do you see new opportunity around every corner?

- Are you accepting the news of the day or do you have your own vision of the world?

- How do you feel when it's raining? Pleased for the plants or miserable because you forgot your umbrella?

The money is already there. The only thing preventing you from being rich is you.

Part 1

Understanding the Basics

'Whatever the mind can conceive and
believe, it can achieve.'

– Napoleon Hill

1

The Science of Attracting Money

'In this infinite sea of potentials that exists around us, how come we keep recreating the same realities?'

– Dr Joseph Dispenza, *The Little Book of Bleeps*

Attracting money can be incredibly easy. There are basically two main steps: understand the scientific theory, then apply it to your own circumstances. (OK, it's not quite that simple, but you still need to know the theory!)

What Do We Mean by 'Money Magnet'?

Have you ever noticed how some people always seem to 'fall on their feet', while others have a different complaint each week?

Have you noticed how people with money find it easy to attract more, while people with little money seem to get less?

Have you noticed that when you feel happy, good things start to happen to you?

Have you ever had a morning where you wake up late, snag your stockings and spill your coffee on your new white blouse ... and you just 'know' that you're going to have a bad day?

These are all examples of the Law of Attraction at work. Just like the law of gravity, the Law of Attraction is a natural law of our universe, and so there is no escaping it. The Law of Attraction states that 'like attracts like'. If you are feeling grumpy, you will attract more reasons to be grumpy. If you are celebrating some good news, you will attract more good news. If you are feeling rich and grateful for all that you have, you will attract more reasons to feel rich and grateful for all that you have.

You are already a magnet, attracting whatever you think about into your life. If you are worrying about the size of the bills you have to pay or whether you can afford to go on holiday this year, you will attract more reasons to worry. Money is likely to become more of a problem. If you feel that life is unfair, it will be unfair.

> The Law of Attraction simply means that 'like attracts like'.

The good news is that once you understand the very simple Law of Attraction, you understand how you can attract more good things into your life. By thinking happy and grateful thoughts, you will attract reasons to be happy and grateful. To be rich, you need to feel rich.

In other words, to attract more wealth into your life, you need to be giving off the 'vibe' of a wealthy person ... and no, this doesn't mean going to buy the latest plasma screen on your credit card!

At this point, you may be tempted to buy a lottery ticket and spend the rest of the week with a big smile on your face as you practise feeling rich. (Don't worry, this is what most people are tempted to do when they first encounter the Law of Attraction.) Unfortunately, you are unlikely to win the lottery. This is because more than 80 per cent of your thoughts are subconscious, and most people have an ingrained limiting belief system about winning lotteries. We will look at limiting beliefs later on in this chapter.

In order to be a Money Magnet, your thoughts and feelings need to be both consciously and unconsciously aligned to the belief that you easily attract money.

Rather than focusing on HOW you will attract money, for example via a big lottery win, it is wiser to focus on feeling wealthy within yourself. Allow yourself to attract money from wherever is easiest for it to reach you. Feeling wealthy within means having high self-esteem and knowing that you are worthy of wealth.

> Being a Money Magnet means finding your 'inner wealth' in order to attract your 'outer wealth'.

Quantum Physics

So how does the Law of Attraction work from a scientific point of view? Just how are your thoughts affecting your reality? Quantum physics provides us with the answers.

You may be familiar with Einstein's equation $E=mc^2$. Quantum physics explains Einstein's theory by telling us that all matter is made up of energy. The chair you're sitting on, the curtain or blind on the window, your clothes, your hands, even your thoughts, are all made up of energy.

Remember when you were at school in the chemistry lab and you got to look through the microscope? Wasn't it amazing how an inanimate object suddenly appeared to be made up of moving cells? Well, in the same way, objects that look solid to our naked eye are actually made up of pure energy vibrating at a certain frequency. The more solid an object is, the lower its frequency of energy.

The Einstein equation $E=mc^2$ was simply a recipe for the amount of energy necessary to create the appearance of mass. It means that there aren't two fundamental physical entities – something material and another immaterial – but only one: energy.

Everything in your world, anything you hold in your hand, no matter how dense, how heavy, how large, on its most fundamental level boils down to

> a collection of electric charges interacting with a background sea of electromagnetic drag force.
>
> – Lynne McTaggart, *The Field*

You Are an Energetic Being

Extend the concept that all matter is effectively a charge of energy and we realise that we too are, in effect, energetic beings. We are energetically connected to everything else. Let's look at some evidence of this.

Kirlian photography shows the existence of coloured energy within and extending outwards from a person. It is often referred to as a person's aura. Some people can actually see the different-coloured auras projected by each person.

In *The Boy Who Saw True* by Cyril Scott, a young boy living in Victorian times describes how he saw a dark greyish aura around one person, which was explained later by the onset of cancer. At the time this boy had no idea that others couldn't see what he could see, but over a period of time he could recognise the significance of each colour that he saw around a person.

If you'd like to see your energetic field, most Mind/Body/Spirit fairs will have someone who can take an aura photograph of you. I recommend that you think happy thoughts beforehand!

Not all of us actually see auras, but most of us sense others' auras as soon as we come into their presence. Think of a person you've met and liked recently. Before you talked with each other, you may have already had a strong feeling that you were going to like this person. Conversely, you may have encountered someone recently who made you want to distance yourself as quickly as possible. These are examples of you 'tuning in' to other people's energy field and even into the pattern of their thoughts. We all do it, and sometimes we describe it as having 'a gut feeling' about someone.

Tapping into the Field

'Aurora', a women's business network in London, hosts regular open evenings. Years ago I attended one of these where the subject of the evening was 'Using Intuition in Business'.

The speaker, an established medium who worked with the police, took the audience of more than 100 business professionals through the following practical exercise:

She wrote the positive qualities of a potential employee on a flipchart on the stage. She then wrote, on the back of the flipchart, one clear reason why we would not employ this employee. We couldn't see the written reason not to employ the person.

She then asked the audience whether, in principle, they would take on this employee and, if not, why not.

No one in the audience had any special psychic skills, and yet many of us – myself included –

'tapped into' something that wasn't visible to our naked eye: that the medium had written a word relating to theft on the back of the flipchart.

Your Thoughts Create Your Reality

Once we understand that our thoughts are energetic threads that can be 'received' by others, it starts to open up a whole new realm of possibility.

Have you ever thought of someone, and seconds later you receive a telephone call from that person? Or you go shopping for a friend's birthday and a certain book falls off the shelf in the shop and you realise that you've found the perfect gift?

You start to discover a link between your thoughts and the reality of your life.

Sometimes it's really obvious, as in the above examples. Other times it is our subconscious at play and the link is less obvious.

However, even if we can't fully explain it, many of us will reach a point where we understand the connections between everything. There are just too many coincidences happening to ignore the possibility of interconnectedness.

Let's look at some simple examples of interconnectedness. As a Feng Shui consultant, I regularly see how a person's home reflects their inner desires and feelings. For example, if the home is cluttered, they are likely to be feeling confused and stuck. If their home is located on the top of a hill, they are likely to be feeling exposed and vulnerable. The outer appearance of the home is a reflection of the 'inner' person who occupies it. They are interconnected. The energy of the home is fully 'mixed up' with the occupant.

One day I watched as a group of people boarded the bus I used to take to school, and I connected to the memory of taking the bus as a young girl and all the feelings attached to it. We are connected to our past as well as to our present and future.

When I decided that I wanted a convertible car with a hard-top roof, even though at the time I didn't know that such a car existed, I was then 'connected' to the newly launched Mercedes SLK. Out of all the different car models on the market, I 'came across' exactly what I was looking for: a convertible with a hard-top roof that went down with the press of a button. Nowadays there are many such models on the road, but at some point a creator had the idea of such a car. He or she connected with the possibility of creating it. Customers like myself connected with the idea of owning such a car, and a new whole new market for the hard-top convertible was born.

Interconnectedness is an exciting concept. It opens up all sorts of possibilities. It makes way for the possibility of miracles. If you are vibrating at a certain frequency, then you will attract the corresponding connection. If you believe in every cell of your body that something is possible, you will connect with that very possibility. Interconnectedness means that nothing happens by accident. We have the chance to be masters of our own lives.

Living in a Realm of Possibilities

Sometimes when we learn something new, it simply raises more questions for us. For example, where did the creator of the hard-top convertible find his or her inspiration? How did the Wright brothers conceive the idea and belief that they could fly in an aeroplane? Where did Mozart find his music? And if we are all energetic beings swimming in a soup of energetic objects, what is this soup that connects us?

Lynne McTaggart, author of *The Field*, refers to the soup as 'The Zero Point'. The Zero Point is described as 'an ocean of microscopic vibrations which appear to connect everything in the universe like some invisible web'. The universe is described in her book as being in a state of infinite possibility. It is the consciousness of the observer that brings an observed object into being. In fact, nothing exists independent of our perception of it. In other words, every minute of every day we are creating our own reality through the concept of interconnectedness.

Bob Proctor, author of *Born Rich* and star of the film *The Secret*, refers to the connecting soup as the 'formless original substance'. In his seminar 'The Science of Getting Rich', Bob outlines the following key truths:

'There is a thinking stuff from which all things are made, and which, in its original state, permeates, penetrates and fills the interspaces of the universe.
'A thought in this substance produces the thing that is imaged by the thought.
'A person can form things in his thought, and by impressing his thought upon formless substance, can cause the thing he thinks about to be created.'

Both Bob Proctor and Lynne McTaggart agree that you are the creator of your world. You have created your current circumstances and you can create new possibilities for yourself.

I like to think of the connecting soup as a space for creation. It offers us the chance of a new possibility. It is where we can create those new energetic possibilities for ourselves.

When we use our energy to think of someone, we create the possibility of seeing them. It is as though our thought has left an imprint in the space which now holds the possibility of it being created. It may take more than just a thought to create the possibility – after all, if the person lives on the other side of the world, it might take a video link or a plane ticket! – but the possibility is there as a result of the thought.

This space is where you will find the possibility of becoming a Money Magnet.

Are You Getting Excited Yet?

If everything is connected energetically and your thoughts hold the power of creation, then you are the main creator of your world. Look around you. Look at your life. Look at how much money you have. What you have in your life is the direct result of your thoughts, whether conscious or subconscious.

Money Mastery

Understanding that you are the master of your life is the secret to attracting whatever you wish. Mastering your thoughts means choosing a direction for your life and keeping your thoughts aligned to that direction. Align your thoughts to attracting more money and you will attract more money. Focus on how little money you have and you will attract even less.

Look at your life and how it is right now. It is the result of your thoughts. If your thoughts are focused on a lack of money, this is what you will attract.

If you are tempted to blame your misfortune on others or on circumstances, such as redundancy, divorce or illness, think again. You are falling into the often delicious temptation of playing the 'victim'. When we play the victim – 'Yes but I was made redundant!', for example – we surrender our power.

It is a tempting role because as the victim we avoid all responsibility. We may even gain sympathy from others.

Can you remember a time when you've played the 'poor me' card? There can be something wondrously addictive about staying in a 'poor me' situation. I know. I've been there. Normally a very positive person, I remember finding myself plunged into the trap of becoming a victim. To illustrate the seductiveness of 'poor me' behaviour, let me share with you my story, telling it first in terms of 'poor me' and then demonstrating how I could have taken responsibility.

'Poor Me'

It started with my decision to invest in a property with an ex-boyfriend, let's call him Alan. As he was skilled in DIY, I thought that his skills and contacts would mean that we could do up the property quickly and fairly cheaply.

We bought the house, half with my cash and the rest with his mortgage, although my name had to go on his mortgage for it to be agreed. The house needed redecorating and a new kitchen and bathroom. Alan seemed keen to get started, so I more or less left him to it.

A few weeks later I arrived at the house to find that the whole of the downstairs floor had been dug out and was now soil! Alan was nowhere to be seen. He wouldn't answer his phone. With no alternative, I contacted the council for advice, hired a skip and then dug out the soil to the required level. It took nearly 10 skips. That's a lot of digging! Alan reappeared when we were nearly finished. I then left him in charge of concreting the floor. As a builder later commented, the concrete floor looked like a replica of the French Alps. Alan disappeared again.

At this point I turned my back on my business and decided to project-manage the rest of the house myself. The trouble was that I was so busy blaming Alan for my circumstances that everything seemed to go wrong. The electrician helped himself to my Dyson vacuum cleaner, the labourer was unreliable and the costs were escalating with no end in sight. Alan then missed a mortgage payment and this caused a problem when I wanted to open a new business account. I had no choice but to cover his mortgage payment. With no income coming in, I was rapidly running out of money. Instead of bringing in friends to help me paint the walls, or paying someone to do it, the 'poor me' had to do it all by myself. With each stroke of paint I reinforced the feeling of 'poor me' in my head, and any savings I had just trickled away.

Even when Alan and his parents turned up to give me a hand, I couldn't let go of the 'poor me' attitude and so, not surprisingly, they weren't too keen to return! Whenever I had the chance I would share my sorry tale with anyone who would listen. It was not my fault that I was running out of money.

Finally my finances forced me to move into the house, and it was at that point that I realised how important it was to shift my energy into a more positive state.

Taking Responsibility

It was my decision to invest with someone who I knew could be unreliable and who was a poor communicator. I agreed to put my name on his mortgage, making me liable should he miss his payments. I didn't take full responsibility for the work to be done on the house. Instead I left it up to Alan. I could have chosen to get in builders much earlier rather than trying to do things on the cheap. If I had spent less energy blaming Alan, I would have had more energy to finish the project within budget. If I could have let go of the anger I was feeling, I would have been able to receive the loving help from him and his parents.

It took me a while to realise that I was playing 'poor me' and, in so doing, I was attracting even more reasons to feel sorry for myself. However, there were benefits in playing the 'poor me': I attracted sympathy and attention from friends. It also meant that I was always right, while Alan was always wrong. This gave me a false sense of 'I'm OK.' It meant that I was blameless for what had happened to me, and so logically I must still be a good person. I also had a good excuse for why my business wasn't doing as well as it could have been. All in all, it was a very seductive package.

All the time that I was blaming Alan, I was not taking responsibility for what I had created in my life. I was angry with him for a long time, and this slowed down progress in other areas of my life. We only have so much energy. If we use it all feeling angry or frustrated or miserable, we have less energy to devote to creating new possibilities. When I finally took responsibility, I bought the house from Alan and was then free to move on to more exciting and lucrative opportunities.

> Blaming others or life's circumstances for your misfortune keeps you where you are, or can even help you to sink further.

In these 'credit crunch' days I am amazed at how much energy is being wasted on blaming the banks and the Government. If a person decides to borrow more money than he can afford, it is his responsibility. Blaming the banks and the Government only creates more of a victim mentality.

Now is the time to realise that you, and you alone, are responsible for your life. Learn from my example above and avoid the victim trap. Resolve to take responsibility for what is in your life. Resolve to shift your focus from a sense of 'lack' to a feeling of richness. If there is anything you don't like in your life, for example insufficient funds in your bank account, then let's start changing that NOW!

■ *Case Study: Jo's Redundancy*

Jo had a good job selling software solutions for a reputable UK company. She was the top salesperson in her team. So when her firm decided to make redundancies and she was one of the few to be made redundant, Jo felt shocked, hurt and very angry.

She took the firm to court for unfair dismissal and reached an out-of-court settlement.

Jo then spent the next two years at home in her dressing gown, telling anyone who'd listen how unfairly she'd been treated.

Catching her off-guard one day, I asked Jo why she had wanted to leave her job. 'Oh' she said, 'I hated going to work. Every morning as I got dressed for work, I'd think to myself, "I really don't want to do this job any more."'

Jo's thoughts created her reality.

Once she accepted that she was responsible for what happened in her life, Jo stopped playing the victim and went on to find herself a new well-paid job and a beautiful home for herself and her daughter.

Unconscious Thoughts

Once you acknowledge your creator role in the energetic pool of your life, everything gets so much easier. Of course, one of the challenges is that the bulk of our thoughts are actually made unconsciously. In order to breathe or to digest our food, we have to have the thought first to create the action. It's just that in the case of breathing, for example, we are unaware of the thought. It happens unconsciously.

More than 80 per cent of our thoughts are unconscious, and so we may be creating, unconsciously, a reality that we don't consciously like.

For example, we want to have lots of money (conscious thought) but maybe we don't actually like rich people (unconscious thought) because at a young age we learned how a wealthy ruler was mean to his people and we then concluded that all wealthy people use their power to be mean to the good people who are poor (unconscious thought).

At some level we will now protect ourselves from being wealthy and mean (unconscious thought) and we may aspire to be poor and good (unconscious thought). Conversely, we may create wealth because we think that, by becoming rich, no one can be mean to us.

Many of us look to wealth for security, and we then create 'just enough' wealth to be secure and have our basic needs met. To have more and to be rich are considered by our unconscious to be 'bad'.

Clearly, the secret is to change your thoughts (conscious and unconscious) in order to create a new possibility for the amount of money in your life. We will look at the proven ways of doing this in Part 2.

Attracting What We (Don't) Want

Jennifer called me, bemoaning the fact she was still single at 36.

'I really want a boyfriend, Marie-Claire. How come I never seem to meet anybody when all my friends are getting married?'

I asked Jennifer to write out two lists for me.

One was a list of all the benefits of being in a relationship, and the other was a list of the benefits of being single.

Needless to say, in Jennifer's case the benefits of being single outweighed those of being married!

Quick Check: Are You a Victim of Circumstances or a Master of Your Money?

* Did something happen to you to create your current financial circumstances?

* Are you wasting your energy on blaming someone else?

* Can you let go of the blame and take full responsibility yourself?

* Is it down to you that you don't have a job, the car of your dreams or enough money in your bank account?

* Can you be OK with that?

* Can you be loving and forgiving of the person who created your current circumstances?

* Are you ready to take full responsibility for what is in your life?

* Are you ready to take full responsibility for the amount of money you are currently attracting?

The money is already there. The only thing preventing you from being rich is you.

2

How Do You Feel About Money?

'Money, the most highly charged word in any language that uses the stuff.'

– Lynn Grabhorn

So now that you are ready to take responsibility for the amount of money in your life and you understand how your thoughts have a direct influence on your circumstances, let's explore how you currently feel towards money.

It's a good idea to be in a safe, quiet place as you read this chapter. This is your opportunity to really get to the heart of what has been holding you back.

You may think that you wish to be rich, but deep down you may feel that being rich is an unsafe place to be. You may have an opinion that rich people can attract jealousy, theft, disloyalty and superficial friends. Maybe it feels much safer for you to stay within a certain income level, where you are less exposed to potential attack. The word 'money' can provoke quite extreme reactions in some people. Many people see a straight choice between being poor and spiritual or being rich and selfish. They flinch at the very mention of 'money'. It is seen as a dirty and even vulgar subject. When I first launched 'How to Become a Money Magnet!' I received some of this negative feedback.

When delivering a workshop or a talk on 'How to Become a Money Magnet!', I often start by congratulating the audience for publicly declaring their desire for more money. If you cannot happily admit to yourself that you wish to be a Money Magnet, you will have a long way to go before you start to attract more money.

I remember participating in a 'Free the Inner Voice' workshop with Nikki Slade. At the start of the workshop, each participant would name their intention for the session. When I announced that my intention was to be rich, it provoked strong reactions. One opera singer, who was later partnered up with me, was clearly appalled. 'As musicians', she explained. 'we perform for pleasure, not for money. The money is unimportant.' I wondered why she took in paying guests to supplement her income, rather than expecting more money from the enormous value she gave others through her singing.

Money Is an Emotional Subject

This chapter is about the emotional connection you have with money. In it, I'll be inviting you to take a good hard look at how you really feel towards money. Your feelings are a clue to your unconscious beliefs. Once you uncover your unconscious blocks to wealth, you will be in a much better position to remove them, should you still wish to do so.

At this point you have a choice. You can either skim through the chapter quickly or you can make a commitment right now to carry out the exercises outlined. Avoiding the exercises is a bit like buying a car and choosing not to drive it. One of the benefits of attending the 'How to Become a Money Magnet!' workshop is that there is no escape from doing the exercises. The results achieved at the workshops prove their value.

If you sincerely wish to shift the level of money that you are currently attracting, I strongly suggest that you complete all the exercises within this chapter. You may be amazed at the insights you'll gain in doing so. All you will need is a pen or pencil, some paper and a quiet space.

Understanding that everything around us is energy, vibrating at different levels, and that like attracts like, you now want to find out how you are currently vibrating on the subject of money. Once you understand your vibration (thoughts and beliefs) about money, you are then in a position to change the frequency!

In all the following exercises it is crucial to be open and honest with yourself. Take the first answer that comes to you and write it down immediately, no matter how strange it may sound to you. It may bring up some emotion for you. You may feel sadness or anger. You may even shed some tears. That's OK. It takes courage to confront your beliefs around money, so be kind and gentle with yourself. It is only by confronting your old beliefs about money that you can start to transform them into more empowering beliefs. It is then that you can become a Money Magnet.

Touching the Money

The following exercise is one that I have used with great success at the 'How to Become a Money Magnet!' workshops. It originally came from some of the people on the workshop and it makes an excellent opener to the tricky subject of money. It can also take you straight to your core beliefs about money.

I am going to ask you four questions.

Before I do so, please can you make sure that you are in a comfortable seating position, where you cannot be easily distracted. Take out a banknote and hold it in your non-writing hand. Have a pen and a blank sheet of paper to hand.

Take three deep breaths and allow your whole body to relax. Clear your mind of any distractions from the day and be still. When you are totally clear and ready, ask yourself the first question and then immediately write down anything that comes into your mind, no matter how ridiculous it may sound.

At your own pace, progress through the four questions. Make sure that you 'clear' your mind and relax fully in between each question. This is a contemplative exercise and not to be rushed.

Are you ready?

Exercise: Touching the Money

Question 1: Money, how do I really feel about you?

Question 2: Money, how do I treat you?

Question 3: Money, how can I have more of you?

Question 4: What else would you like to tell me, money?

OK, how was that for you? Did you discover some clarity?

Did you uncover any surprises or interesting insights about your feelings towards money? Don't worry if you haven't received an amazing revelation just yet. Just doing this exercise in itself opens you to the possibility of attracting more money.

If you are not sure whether you have done the exercise correctly, don't worry. There are no correct answers. Just allow your answers to come from your heart rather than your head. This is not an intellectual exercise. Whatever you have written is a reflection of your thoughts around money. It is your truth. However, to give you some examples, here are my answers from the very first time I did this exercise many years ago.

Question 1: Money, How Do I Really Feel About You?

'Disposable, purple, glittering silver, precious, loved, plentiful, not to be defaced or abused, handled by many'

Question 2: Money, How Do I Treat You?

'With love and respect. With joy. With gratitude, sometimes a little embarrassed, with pride, sometimes too boastful. Carelessly at times. Trusting. Cavalier'

Question 3: Money, How Can I Have More of You?

'Smile more, go out more, love more, give more, share more. Believe in me. Rejoice for life is plentiful. Plan to have more money. Accept money. Greet money like a good friend.'

Question 4: What Else Would You Like to Tell Me, Money?

'Don't be afraid of having more; you are good enough. Think Big. Give Big. Accept Big Rewards of Money. Money is good. It is holy. It is love. It is a thank you. Love is energy and you have lots of it.'

Remember, the above responses are just examples, not instructions. You will find your own words and inspiration. You will uncover your own truths about money.

With this initial exercise you are starting to tap into what you really think about money. Of course, the tricky bit is that at least 80 per cent of your thoughts are subconscious.

While you may consciously wish to be rich, your subconscious may hold what it considers to be good evidence that being rich doesn't actually make you happy. In such an example, your subconscious is keeping you from being unhappy. Your subconscious thoughts could be 'protecting' you from feeling rich!

(Don't forget, it's only acting on information received and is doing its best!)

Clearly you need to uncover more about your current thought patterns on money, so that you can change them, quickly!

You will now be building up a clearer idea of your true thoughts about money from the exercise above. Let's build on that by exploring your beliefs on money a little further.

Money Stories and Sayings

It is crucial that you don't cheat with this exercise by including any preparation beforehand or by turning the page to look at others' answers. Doing so would weaken the power of any insights gained. For the following exercise you will need a blank piece of paper that you can cut or tear into smaller strips of paper.

Exercise: Money Beliefs

Jot down quickly any thoughts that come to mind about money, ideally each one on a separate piece of paper. Use the questions below as a prompt.

What were you told as a child about money?

What did money mean to you as you were growing up?

What's your favourite saying about money?

What comes to mind when you read about wealthy people?

Who is your role model for attracting money? Describe the person.

Then divide the pieces of paper into two piles, one representing positive statements and the other representing negative statements.

If you have more negative than positive statements, it offers an explanation as to why you are attracting less money than you wish. You are literally vibrating at a frequency that will only attract a limited amount of money.

Please complete this exercise BEFORE reading further. You can simply read the book, but you increase your chance of success by doing the exercises in it!

If you have more positive statements than negative and you are still unhappy with the amount of money in your life, we simply need to raise the bar – we'll start doing this in Part 2.

Here are some of the most common beliefs about money heard on the 'How to Become a Money Magnet!' workshops. Not surprisingly, the list of negative money beliefs was longer than the list of positive money statements!

Don't beat yourself up if you've carried on reading without completing the exercise. Give yourself a break. Take some time out now to quickly jot down how you feel about money. Respond to the questions in the previous exercise. It will only take you a few minutes and it could pave the way to a more abundant life.

If you keep rushing through life, you risk missing the most important bits. You miss hearing your inner voice. You'll mistake external circumstances and other people's opinions for the truth. Many of our beliefs about money stem from our families, our national and religious heritage, our friends and our colleagues. Take some time to listen in to what beliefs you have taken on board. Isn't it time to take a moment to listen to you?

Congratulations if you completed the exercise before reading on! Your commitment to becoming a Money Magnet will lead to faster results.

Below you will find some of the responses from people who've attended the 'How to Become a Money Magnet!' workshop. It will be interesting to compare your responses and look out for any common themes. Very often our beliefs about money come from what we were told as children. Can you remember who educated you first about money? What did they teach you was the most important thing about money? Was it important to enjoy it or to save it? Were you expected to work hard for your money or were you taught that you'd always be looked after?

These beliefs are accepted at a young age as being the truth. Now is the time to flush out these learned beliefs. Then you can go on to decide for yourself whether these are empowering beliefs or not. You can then consciously select only the positive beliefs about money that will transform you into a Money Magnet.

Negative Statements about Money

'Money doesn't grow on trees.'

'It is easier for a camel to pass through the eye of a needle than for a rich man to enter the kingdom of heaven.'

'Filthy rich.'

'It's impolite to discuss money.'

'There's never enough money.'

'We can't afford it.'

'I never have enough.'

'Only the rich get rich and the poor get poorer.'

'Born with a silver spoon.'

'You don't get something for nothing!'

'You have to work hard to be rich.'

'Money is the root of all evil.'

'I hate taxes.'

'True wealth has nothing to do with money.'

Positive Statements about Money

'I am a Money Magnet!'

'I've always been lucky.'

'I'm good at what I do.'

'I deserve to be rich.'

'Money buys you time.'

Yup, that was it ... don't worry, we'll help you find some more in Part 2!

'Money for Money's Sake'

Listening to many of the negative statements about money over the years, I've found that the general consensus is that 'money for money's sake' is not a good thing.

The Bible's proclamation about the rich man and the camel through the eye of a needle suggests that the pursuit of money for money's sake can distract us from what is really important, and I agree. But you can still be a Money Magnet. It's just all about the 'vibe' that you're giving out!

Have you ever noticed how some people just seem to behave in a confident way, whereas others have their heads bowed? Which type of behaviour do you think is most likely to attract financial opportunities and lucky breaks?

Thanks to Facebook, I have recently renewed contact with one of the telesales staff that I used to manage. As I remember him, Vince was an average performer with high expectations of himself and immense self-confidence. I was not surprised to hear that he has gone on to make a huge success of his life. Don't look to your current circumstances, look to your thoughts and expectations.

> Wanting money just to have money is not healthy and will rarely work.

If you feel you don't deserve to be rich, you never will be, even if you win the lottery. Look at the many people who have won millions on the lottery, only to let it slip through their fingers in no time at all, often resulting in being worse off than previously.

Winning the Lottery

Winning the lottery is what most people think of when they think of attracting money. They are focused on the money, and often on the huge unlikelihood of actually winning! It's not surprising then that they fall at the first hurdle. However, you can use the idea of winning the lottery as a way to discover what you really want from life. By imagining what it would be like to FEEL like a lottery winner, you have a way to discover why you WANT to be a Money Magnet and why you DESERVE to be a Money Magnet. Holding a vision of what you would do with money is a far more efficient way of attracting money than focusing on the money itself.

Let me share with you the story of Susie. Susie came along to Miracle Club (the local coaching group I'd set up by myself) with a strong identity of 'poor me'. 'Life just wasn't fair' for Susie. She'd been trying to get pregnant with no success, and she couldn't see the point of life if she couldn't have a baby. She had no other interests or passions. She didn't have a job and, when her husband was made redundant, money became a big issue in the household. Susie joined a syndicate lottery group.

I asked Susie to write down what she would do if she won £10 million. Her answers revealed a completely different side to Susie, and she has graciously allowed me to share them with you here.

What Susie Would Do with £10 Million

- Drink only the best champagne a couple of times a week and send champagne, chocolates and flowers to others at random, either through the post or in person.

- Treat everyone who has been there for me (as I have been a bit difficult and down over the last five years) to a fab spa holiday once a year; hold several really lovely soirées with champagne, cocktails and canapés; take taxis home or to a 5-star hotel; organise a big rave-up with a marquee on our lawn.

- Celebrate 10 years of happy marriage to my darling husband by having a fab party on our lawn just like our wedding, except I would like to be more sober this time!

- Pay mortgages off for special people including family, friends and random others!

- Pay for the utmost security or guards to look after my parents' two houses as they were burgled again last night.

- Treat my family to some luxury.

- Obviously treat my husband to all his team's football matches and to meet all the players (yawn).

- Send my husband and dad, and anyone else who thinks they have been hard done by, around the world for 80 days.

- Arrange Feng Shui and life coaching with Marie-Claire for all my good friends and family.

- Try to stop crime and try to return stolen stuff back to the victims for whom the greatest loss may be its sentimental value, which means nothing to those who've stolen it. Introduce some amazing system. Try to discourage the practice in the first place! Try to make it less attractive to steal.

- Support and fund some of those businesspeople who dare to go on *Dragons' Den* to attract funding.

- Return to Fiji, the Maldives and Cyprus and lie on sun-kissed beaches with friends and family, just chilling and having a good time.

- Go to Byron Bay for a couple of months and perhaps build a house (half my brother's ashes are there, as that's where we lost him, and that was his dream). Put lots of benches around the place dedicated to him and my granddad and other members of the family.

- Promote meditation, relaxation and Marie-Claire-type of courses to get people to a better place.

- Provide education to those who really need it.

- Support and invest in Marie-Claire's vision of 'Miracle Club'.

- Have a cleaner and cook and gardener, or pay for lovely easy lessons to learn how to do these things properly!

- Get a hot tub for the garden and a new shed with lots of windows to enjoy the view.

- Provide the best possible counselling service for people I know who may need it.

- Set up charities for what I think are worthwhile causes, such as animal charities. Make a huge pot of money available for people who cannot afford fertility treatment and for websites that people actually set up for no benefit to themselves other than to help other people (such as the one that saved my life about fertility).

- Make the concept of The Secret Millionaire become part of everyday life.

- Sponsor all the people who ask me.

- Pay for a few more fertility treatments and help my wonderful IVF friends and others who have sacrificed lots for the dream that others take for granted.

- Provide taxis for people who really need them.

- Provide meals out for people who really need them and not just homeless people.

- Become a member of a local club or interest group that intrigues me – and stop the 'Poor Me' game!

- Share things with lovely people.

- Stop animal and people cruelty (now you are all really worried, but I am a multi- millionaire!).

- Have a boat somewhere lovely – and a private jet and helicopter.

- Have a fab but realistically modest party with you lot from Miracle Club once a year!

- Provide somewhere for teenagers to go.

- Provide hope for people where it's lacking.

In reading Susie's list, did you pick up on her excitement as she envisaged all that she was capable of doing with her life? Did you notice how long it took before Susie mentioned IVF and fertility treatments?

The list reveals a very loving person with a lot to give the world. It also brought up strong passions and ideas, some of which were a surprise to Susie. With or without the £10 million, Susie realised she already had a lot more in her life that she had imagined. In taking time to envisage the possibilities, Susie found more direction and purpose. She also had great fun in fantasising her dream life.

The more we can enjoy the feeling of having money, the more we are likely to attract it.

Now it's your turn. Enjoy this exercise. It's fun to play make-believe!

Exercise: The Lottery List

If you won £10 million on the lottery, what would you spend it on, honestly?

....

....

....

....

....

....

....

....

....

....

....

Would your money disappear as quickly as it arrived?

Would you live your life differently?

How would money empower you?

How would you being rich benefit the world?

HINT: If you no longer needed to get out of bed in the morning, your life would be the poorer for it (life is about living, not sleeping!).

The Value of Money

- How much do you value your money?

- Do you work hard for your money or does it come to you easily?

- Are you cautious in your spending or do you like to splash out once in a while?

- Do you know how much money is in your wallet right now?

- What are your feelings about the cash in your wallet?

- Is it enough?

- Do you feel wealthy?

How you feel about money will have an effect on how much of it you attract. The more grateful you are for the money you have, the more money you are likely to attract.

Lynn Grabhorn, author of *Excuse Me, Your Life Is Waiting*, shares a tip in her book on how to increase the perceived value of money in your wallet:

'Imagine that you have £100 in your wallet. It may be your last £100 for the month. You may be suffering from a feeling of "lack", particularly if you start to consider everything that the £100 won't be able to buy you. When you are coming from a position of "lack", you are focusing on all that you can't afford and on how little money you have. As

like attracts like, your thoughts of "lack" will only attract further drains on your income.'

Instead, you need to shift your focus. You need to start valuing the money that you do have. To do this, Lynn recommends that you take the £100 that you have got and, instead of thinking what it won't buy, start thinking about what it could buy.

Imagine walking down a high street ... how many books could you buy with £100? What item of clothing could you buy for a £100, maybe a new pair of jeans and a couple of smart shirts? What gifts could you buy to treat a loved one? Maybe you'd fancy an indulgent massage, a meal for two or a session with a life coach?

Explore as many different choices as you can. Be aware of how your body posture may change as you do so. You are feeling happier and more confident. You start to appreciate the level of control and choice that you can have with your money. You start to appreciate its value. These appreciative thoughts and feelings for money will then start to attract more money.

> What you focus on, you will attract.
>
> Value the money that you have and you will attract more of it.

The 'energetic' link between money and value was born in the concept of exchange. Money was created as a convenient way to exchange goods of differing values.

Most people value their money more if they have worked hard for it. The money is perceived as a fair exchange for the amount of work undertaken. If you work full-time, you would expect to receive a regular income. However, if you are constantly late to work or you are delivering poor results, you are not appreciating the value of your salary. The likely result will be less money, or you may even lose your job.

▪ *Case Study: Spending Money Like Water*

There was a time in my life when I was earning a lot of money but I didn't value the amount of money I was earning. Although I had worked hard to earn it, I had now reached a plateau where I could coast a little at work, thanks to the foundations I'd laid. At this point, the money suddenly seemed to be excessive compared to the reduced amount of effort I was putting in.

I couldn't spend it fast enough. I spent it on all the usual things like a smart flat and a fast sports car, but my biggest indulgence was art. I bought several paintings at £2,000, and I still have one Derek Hare original that I bought from Harrods for £8,000. That was particularly profligate, as by then I knew Derek personally and I could have bought it direct from him – and probably at a lower price as he'd be keeping all the profits!

Now I understand how lottery winners go through their winnings so quickly!

If you don't value how you receive the money, you won't value the money.

When you receive money in exchange for something you value, like your home or your car, you are likely to value the money received. If your home or car is no longer loved or appreciated, this may lower your expected value of it, and in turn the money you receive for it. The amount you value your money can be directly proportionate to the amount that you value what you have provided in exchange for the money. Ultimately, the more you value yourself, with all your unique gifts and qualities, the more value you will expect to receive.

Love yourself and money will love you too.

It is easier to believe that you can have more money in your life if you feel that you deserve to receive more and if you feel that you have more to offer the world. The amount of money you have is a reflection of the amount of value you have for yourself.

Value Yourself More

My friend Alison and I were recently discussing whether or not to attend a talk on 'Discovering Your Purpose'. I realised then that we all share a common purpose in life. Our purpose is simply to find the love within us. If everybody on the planet found the love within, we would all radiate love and the world would be transformed. There would be no place for greed or violence or poverty. We would live in abundance.

'Finding the Love Within' ...

... means following your heart more than your head.

It means following your passions and living a life that you love.

It means feeling safe but honouring your desire to grow and to seek new horizons.

It means allowing yourself to blossom into your full potential.

It means connecting with your birthright of abundance.

When you value and love yourself, you are wealthy and you will attract wealth.

Now, you may be saying to yourself 'I do value myself, so why am I not attracting more money into my life?' Before we go on to look at your precise beliefs about money, let's take a moment to look at where you could be valuing yourself more.

First of all, you are the expert on you. When you complete the following exercise, trust that you have all the right answers within you, and they will come. If you feel some resistance, take a break for a cup of tea and then come back to the exercise. If you are not sure how you are failing to value yourself, take a look at anyone you know whom you judge to be neglecting themselves. They will serve as a valuable mirror to show you what you are not seeing in yourself.

For example, I once shared a home with a man who showed very little respect for his health. He drank excessive amounts of alcohol, smoked cigarettes and lived on takeaways. I couldn't understand how he could be a mirror for me, when I ate a mostly raw-food diet, only drank alcohol occasionally and had given up smoking years previously. When I looked a little closer, though, I realised that over the years I had put on quite a bit of weight and that I rarely exercised. Like him, I had in fact been neglecting my health. I had to thank him for holding up a mirror to my own state, and I drastically reviewed my eating habits, bought a bicycle and joined a gym as a result.

Are you valuing yourself in terms of your health, the work you do and in the relationships that you have? Are you choosing activities that you love to do? Does your body really love watching TV or would it rather be enjoying a walk or chatting with friends? Are you allowing others to love you? How are you demonstrating respect for yourself on a daily basis?

Complete the exercise below for some powerful insights into how you currently value yourself. This will put you in a great position for when we return to this subject in more depth in Part 2.

<u>Exercise: Increasing Your Self-Worth</u>

Write down five ways in which you are not valuing yourself. What could you do differently?

....

....

....

....

....

Write down five ways in which you currently value yourself. How could you do more to value yourself?

....

....

....

....

....

Well done on completing the previous exercise. I salute your courage in being prepared to take a good hard look at yourself and at your level of self-worth. You are well on your way to clearing out any resistance to attracting more money.

You are now ready to look at any specific limiting beliefs that you are harbouring towards money itself. Remember, your thoughts create your reality. Even though you may express a strong conscious desire for more money, you may be holding on to some very good reasons to push money away. By shedding some light on these barriers to your wealth, you'll then be in a position to 'kick them over' and get back on your pathway to riches.

Why are you not attracting more money into your life?

Take a pen and write down in the space below all the benefits of having LESS money. (In a moment you'll read about some of the responses collected from people on the 'How to Become a Money Magnet' workshops, but try not to look before you have completed the exercise yourself.)

Exercise: The Benefits of Having LESS Money in My Life

....

....

....

....

....

....

....

....

....

....

If you're struggling with the above exercise, try this next one. In fact, try it anyway!

Exercise: The Problems with Having LOTS of Money

....

....

....

....

....

....

....

....

....

....

Can you think of any more good reasons to have less money in your bank account? Sometimes it's not the first things that come to mind, but the ideas that arrive almost as an afterthought that are the most insightful.

This very powerful exercise will help you to find what has been in the way of you becoming a Money Magnet.

From the Workshops: Some Benefits of Having LESS Money in Your Life

Be more creative: boot sales, homemade cards, bartering of services

Pay less for items; become expert bargain-hunter

Less waste

Fewer costs

Fewer/no taxes

Fewer responsibilities

Less admin

Nicer person

Mix with nicer people

More spiritual: 'I am always provided for'

Avoids being honest when we say 'no'; instead we use 'I can't afford to'

Receive more gifts

Loved for who I am

Fewer bad habits as can't afford them!

Share more, e.g. car journeys

The Problems with Having LOTS of Money

People only love you for your money

Fewer real friends, shallow friendships

Distances you from your 'roots'

Lose touch with reality

No sense of purpose

Added responsibilities

Need to employ accountants, etc.

More admin

More tax

Inheritance issues

Problem of choice: which car, which home?

In the public arena

Security and fear of extortion

Choice

Charity demands

Less time, less privacy

The Power of Belief

By now you should be gaining some real insights into how you really feel about the subject of money and, as a result, why you have as much or as little money as you do in the bank.

Your beliefs are so powerful. They direct your unconscious thought patterns, which in turn create your reality.

I remember a time in my life when I was trying to get my coaching consultancy up and running. I was achieving superb results with the few clients that I did attract, but there seemed to be a ceiling on how many new clients I could sign up in a month. I also seemed to have a block about charging the full price for the coaching, so I would often offer a 50 per cent discount. I'd even had leaflets printed offering 50 per cent off all my coaching services!

I had to take a close look at my belief systems. I found that because I was naturally good at the coaching, it required less effort or preparation for me than, say, delivering a talk or preparing a Feng Shui consultation. I was valuing what I did in terms of the effort required to do it, rather than the benefit that I was offering my clients. Once I looked at how just four weeks of coaching could literally transform somebody's life, I felt OK about increasing the value of my offering – and I started to attract more clients.

I was still hitting a barrier in terms of income, however, so I looked even more closely at the beliefs that I held around earning money. I also looked at the behaviour of the people around me, and compared it with my own. And I realised, with some degree of dismay, that I absolutely loved to get things at a bargain, or even for free. I was associating having less money with being more creative, having more friends and, all in all, with being a much nicer person. In fact, many people had given me feedback, back in my high-earning sales director days, that I had not really been a particularly nice person. So, in my mind, I had associated earning lots of money with not being a good person. Everybody loves to be loved, and so my limiting belief was that to be loved, I had to remain at a limited income level. Hmm.

Eventually, after lots of thought, I realised that I just needed to find the love within, as mentioned earlier.

Remaining a prisoner to your beliefs limits your power to become a Money Magnet. Taking responsibility for what is in your life, and the beliefs that created it, is the route to freedom and abundance.

Look at some of the beliefs that you wrote down earlier. What would your life be like without them? Is there one belief that stands out above all the rest? Is there a general theme to your limiting beliefs? Maybe a thought that you don't love yourself enough to earn more, or that you're just not worth a higher income?

When they have gone through these exercises and had an opportunity to discuss how they feel towards money, people on the 'How to Become a Money Magnet!' workshop invariably 'boil it down' to one single limiting belief about money. This one belief is having the biggest impact on why they are not attracting more money into their lives. If removed, this would have the most noticeable and immediate effect on how much money then started to flow their way. So what about you?

Is there one belief holding you back most from attracting money? What is it?

Write it here, as you may need to refer back to it when reading Part 2.

The one belief holding me back from attracting money is:

....

....

....

....

In running the 'How to Become a Money Magnet!' workshop with hundreds of students, we found that there was one common belief statement for most of us. This does not preclude other beliefs, but it does suggest that most of us carry a similar burden. This belief is that:

'I am not good enough.'

Does that resonate with you? Is there part of you nodding in agreement, even if another part of you is protesting? Is your head responding in one way and your heart another? What does it mean to you to think, 'I am not good enough'? Does it mean that you are not worthy? Or that you don't love yourself enough? Does it mean you're not worth the going rate, or that your colleagues deserve to be paid more than you? Does it mean that you don't value yourself or what you do any more? Does it mean that, inside of you, you know that you're no longer giving your best effort? Does it mean that you are resigned to your fate – that you have given up? Does it mean that you will never be good enough so there's no longer any point in trying? Maybe somebody told you a long time ago that you were not good enough and you took that comment on board as though it was the truth.

The lower your self-value, the lower your attraction for money.

Explore how your body is feeling right now. Your body is the key to unlocking your truths. For example, when I wrote the last sentence of the last paragraph, I felt what could only be described as an 'inner laugh' within my body. On questioning this, I realised it's because I'd been struck by the ridiculousness of accepting a comment from years long ago as the truth. In that moment of realisation, I released whatever I had been hanging on to for years without even knowing it.

This is powerful work. Tread gently, but don't run away from it. Your limiting beliefs can only keep you prisoner if you turn your back on them. Face them full-on and the chains that have been holding you back so far will release you. As well as a sense of release through laughter, you may also experience the emotional release of tears. That's OK, too. Give yourself the space to let go.

Letting go of any belief that you are not good enough is the gateway to the life of your dreams.

One note of caution: Beware of distractions, such as suddenly feeling the need to go and eat something at this stage of the book. From personal experience I know that some of you will try to avoid your real emotions by stuffing them back down again with food. Delay the temptation to eat (or drink or smoke or telephone a friend, or whatever is your favourite distraction) until you've finished this chapter. If that brings up another reaction in you, such as anger, that's OK, too. Question what you are really angry about?

Grab a piece of paper and start a written conversation between you and your emotions. Remember, the power to transform your wealth is within you. It is time to get to know the real you and to flush out all the 'clutter' of your limiting beliefs. Your emotions act as signposts along the way. Trust them and question them to find your answers. Only you have access to your truth. Nobody can do this for you. It is time to trust yourself.

Letting go of any belief that you are not good enough is the gateway to the life of your dreams. Don't worry if you're not sure whether you've released anything yet, as we cover this subject in much more depth in Part 2.

Congratulations on reaching this point of awareness.

Recognise that a low sense of self-worth is lowering your 'money vibration'. In holding on to your limiting beliefs, you are resisting the opportunity of having a rich and successful life.

■ *Case Study: Money as an Indicator of Perceived Value*

As UK sales director of a software company, I was responsible for delivering more than £18 million sales each year. In return, I was paid a very generous six-figure salary. It was a fair exchange.

Then I reached a point where I no longer believed that I was worth the latest pay rise; I had trained up the sales team and their managers to the extent that they no longer needed my daily support, and the sales targets were being achieved with less and less input from me. Although my boss was happy, I felt that I was no longer giving value in exchange for my salary.

When the company started to consider a few redundancies, I became increasingly embarrassed about the size of my salary. I reasoned that I could save at least three people's jobs if I were to leave. I no longer appreciated the value of my role in the company, even though it was still valued by others.

Instead of looking at the results, I judged my personal value by the effort required to do the job. With less effort required, I valued myself less. In the end, my limiting belief could no longer sustain the large salary and I left the job.

We can only attract what we believe we are worth.

In Part 2 we'll look at proven ways to transform your low-level vibration so that you start to become a Money Magnet!

■ Case Study: How Your Feelings May Be Blocking the Flow of Money

Andrea called me, as she was feeling poor. On paper Andrea was a successful PR consultant, but she never seemed to have enough money at the end of the month.

During the course of the consultation I discovered why Andrea might have unconsciously been resisting the money in her life. Instead of focusing on her successes, Andrea was feeling huge guilt about having to put her grandmother into a nursing home. This meant that on some level she didn't feel worthy of the good in her life.

Once we'd identified the cause, it was relatively easy to clear it using some of the methods that I'll describe in Part 2.

Within six months of the consultation, Andrea was able to accept that her grandmother really was getting the best care and that she shouldn't keep beating herself up about it. Andrea is now a Money Magnet!

Checklist

- Do you feel that you still have blocks to receiving more money?

- Name your biggest resistance to wealth.

- Are you ready to let it go?

- Are you ready to step outside your comfort zone?

- Can you imagine being wealthy?

- What would it mean to you?

- What could you afford to do with money that you can't do now?

- What could you start now in anticipation of the money?

- How can you show yourself more love and respect?
- How can you increase your value?

The money is already there.
The only thing preventing you from
being rich is you.

3

How Much Money?

- How much money would you like to have?
- How much money do you actually have, right now?
- Do you know? Do you have at least a vague idea?

If you don't know where the starting line is, you won't be in the best position to run the race.

Some would disagree with me here. After all, you want to attract more money into your life, so what does it matter where you start from?

We don't include balance sheets on the 'How to Become a Money Magnet!' workshops, but in my own experience, taking time to 'face up' to your money is all part of conquering any limiting beliefs that you have around money and its influence on your life.

■ Case Study: Know How Much Money You Want!

After attending the one-day 'How to Become a Money Magnet!' workshop, Emma went home with a fresh view on money. She was no longer afraid of it. I'll let Emma continue telling her story:

'On Tuesday last week I sat down with my husband to work out how much money we needed for Christmas to cover all the entertaining and presents. It totalled £1,000. We had not saved at all and I usually get a bonus in November, but the company has changed the payout to February next year. Usually I would have worried about where the money would come from, but this time I didn't – after all, I am a Money Magnet!

'I have been de-cluttering my house for the past couple of weeks, and finances was top priority for Friday night. During the Money Magnet workshop my limiting belief was that I feared money, and subsequently had not been opening my bank statements for months. I went through our joint account and, to my amazement, we had exactly £1,000 to spare – we had still been paying money in for an old credit card direct debit.

'What is more astonishing is that when we had to answer "Money, what else would you like to tell me?" my answer was, "I'm waiting for you and I have been for a while."'

It's time to make friends with money and to find out how strong a magnet you really are to money. Remember, the results in our lives are the most accurate way of measuring the pattern of our thoughts, both conscious and unconscious.

Without checking your accounts, complete the chart on page 59.

Now complete it accurately, referring to any relevant papers or accounts. For some of you, getting accurate figures may involve clearing out drawers-full of old papers.

Clear space to do it now.

Need an incentive?

The last time I checked my accounts, I found a large investment in Premium Bonds that I'd completely forgotten about. Sounds ridiculous? Have a go yourself and see what you can find.

Exercise: 'My Money Bank' Chart

Current Account(s)

Savings Account(s)

Shared Account(s)

Mortgage Account (equity)

Internet Account

Premium Bonds

Shares

Property Investments

Business Investments

Other investments

Piggy bank

Monies owed to me

Have You Found All Your Money Yet?

Do you know that when they construct lists of the wealthiest people in the world, the newspapers will normally calculate the person's net wealth to include the value of their various investments including property and businesses?

What's your total worth? Are you feeling wealthier yet?

> Some of you may find that you are millionaires already and you didn't even know it!

■ Case Study: Finding the Money

My Reiki master, Jake, had recommended that I attend Diana Cooper's month-long residential course. This was in 2003 and the cost of the course was £2,000. I told Jake that I would only go if I 'happened' to find the money.

A couple of days later I was clearing through my papers and I found an old account with £3,000 in it.

How Much Are You Currently Attracting?

If you have been focusing on the lack of money in your life, this is the moment where you shift your focus.

Again, you may need to double-check your papers as well as your memory. In addition to any regular dependable income you receive each month, maybe from different sources, I'd like you to remember any times in the last six months when you have attracted money from somewhere else. This could have been a gift, a tip, a bonus or an extra opportunity for which you have received money e.g. babysitting, selling goods on eBay, commission on a one-off brokered deal or some after-hours training for a colleague. Many of my clients regularly find money literally lying in the street! Have you 'accidentally' found any cash in the last few months?

◼ *Case Study: Attracting Money Easily*

When you are a Money Magnet, money is easily attracted to you when you need it.

I had the money to pay for Diana Cooper's course, but ideally I wanted to attract enough money to cover my monthly mortgage payment while I was away.

One week later I received a call from a friend enquiring about a place for another friend to rent while he waited to move house.

The friend rented my home for exactly one month while I was away on my course.

I was a Money Magnet!

Create Your Own 'I Attract Money' Chart

Regular Income

salary: full-time

salary: part-time

property rental incomes

income from shares

Additional Income

gifts or inheritance

state benefit

through the sale of private items

one-off projects

temporary jobs

'discovered' cash, on streets or in forgotten accounts

money back on goods purchased

free money with a loyalty card

I LOVE getting FREE money off my shopping at some supermarkets!

Needless to say, the above lists are not for accounts or tax purposes. They are for your eyes only, as we assess the current strength of your Money Magnet.

As your mind expands to the many different ways in which you can attract money into your life, you will start to notice even more and, bit by bit, the power of your magnet will grow.

■ *Case Study: Being Open to All Opportunities*

For readers in the UK, check out Martin's Money Tips. Thanks to his advice, I made one phone call and wrote one letter to my old mortgage company. One week later I received a cheque for £175!

Even better, my friend Nick followed Martin's advice and recovered a total of £14,000 in refunded bank charges!

www.moneysavingexpert.com

Real Money and 'Pretend' Money

In today's credit-crazed society, it can be tricky simply spending your own money and not someone else's. If you've ever owned a credit card, you'll know the experience of 'paying' for something without feeling like you're really parting with any cash. It's easy to up your spending on the spur of the moment to something more expensive. After all, it's not as though you have to find the extra cash in your pockets or do an extra couple of hours' work first! Add to the buying process the huge stimuli of advertising, and it's not surprising that credit cards are at the root of most of today's money problems.

During a period of no regular fixed income, I remember realising that I had access to nearly 50 per cent of my home's value on credit cards! Having access to so much liquid cash would be enough for anyone to believe that they were financially OK, and I was no exception. My credit cards enabled me to benefit from many amazing learning experiences and a couple of holidays, when in reality I didn't have the money to pay for them.

This is what I refer to as attracting 'pretend' money. It is not the same as making a conscious decision to borrow money for a specific purpose. It is living beyond your means, and it does not come into the remit of being a Money Magnet.

Credit Where Credit Is Due

If you use credit cards, take the time now to check how much debt you have. Yes, 'debt' is a nasty word, acting like a drain on your magnetic energies. It's like filling up a bucket with money, only to discover that you're leaking (those'll be the interest payments) out of the bottom!

Act on your debt now in order to plug that hole!

■ Case Study: Attracting 'Pretend' Money

Following one of my talks in Liverpool, a journalist approached me with a private question. She described how she had needed to 'attract' £2,000 in order to pay off her credit card. She had followed most of the guidelines that I'd shared earlier with the audience, but it hadn't worked. Instead of attracting £2,000 into her bank account, she'd ended up with £2,000 more on her credit card debt! She wanted to know where she'd gone wrong.

I asked her how she had asked for the £2,000. 'Oh' she answered casually, 'I simply thought "Wouldn't it be lovely if I had £2,000 for my credit card?"'

We'll look later at how important it is that we are clear with our words!

Somewhere in your subconscious, debt will hold you back from being a true money magnet, so take the following actions, where appropriate:

Fixing the Hole in Your Bucket

- Pay off all outstanding credit card balances each month.

- Always pay off more than the minimum payment each month.

- Pay off the balances with the highest interest rate first.

- Look at transferring high-rate balances to a low-rate or o per cent card (check the transfer fee and the rate for any incumbent balance on the low-rate card).

- Keep a close check on your financial status each month.

- If you are struggling, get some help: negotiate with the credit card companies.

- Look to spend less and attract more real money!

Money Magnets and Spending

■ Case Study: A Friend's Advice

Doing my accounts one day many years ago, I realised that I had heavily overspent during the previous 12 months. Bemoaning my fate, I asked my good friend Karen for advice.

'Well,' she said, 'it's easy! You either have to spend less or earn more.'

That time I took the second option and changed jobs to attract more money.

Money is your friend. It enables you to be who you really want to be. And yet many of us keep money at a distance. Start making friends with money again, and spend a week using only cash.

Some proponents of the Law of Attraction emphasise that it's good to spend your money whenever you wish to. They present the case that 'If you act like a wealthy person, you'll be vibrating as one and will therefore attract more wealth into your life.' To some extent that may be true.

Exercise

Spend a week using only cash to pay for everything.

If you are spending money which you know, on some level, you don't have, this will not work. Remember, it is not so much the conscious thought – for example, 'I feel wealthy indulging in this treat' – as the unconscious thought 'I shouldn't really be spending this money right now' that creates your financial reality.

I once rented a beautiful apartment before I had a way of paying for it. I attracted a job soon afterwards, but when the job disappeared, I carried on living in the apartment, acting 'as if' I could afford it. Of course, my savings dried up and in the end I had to face reality and move out.

How Would a Wealthy Person Think?

To vibrate as a Money Magnet, it helps if we adopt some of the behaviours of wealthy people. Most wealthy people I know count the pennies and let the pounds look after themselves.

Did you hear about Duncan Bannatyne, the self-made millionaire who is one of the dragons from the TV series *Dragons' Den*? Despite his incredible wealth and the success of his companies, Duncan once asked his staff not to purchase any paperclips – he reckoned they could save money by collecting paperclips from the morning's post instead!

How do the wealthy approach spending? The answer is, creatively.

Exercise: Spending Creatively

Before we can get creative, we need to know how much we are playing with.

Do you know how much money you actually spend?

If you are not sure, carry out these initial steps first and start to spend time with your new friend, money:

- Carry a notepad with you for a week to monitor your spending.

- Transfer all your spending totals into a monthly expenditure chart (an Excel spreadsheet is a big help with this).

- Gather similar items into groups, such as: regular bills, entertainment, miscellaneous.

- Select a number of key items from the list, as it's now time to get creative and to think like a Money Magnet.

When I looked at my various expenditure items, I soon realised where I was overspending in a few areas:

Expenditure Item	Small action	OK action	Significant action
Petrol	Check prices on web	Share lifts to work	Buy a lower-emission car
Lunch	Take packed lunch	Eat less!	Change jobs for one with a canteen
Books	Use the library	Share books with friends	Donate books to charity shops (and maybe pick up one or two as well!)

- For each of your expenditures, come up with a creative way of having the item but spending less, thereby leaving you more money in your bank account. Start thinking like Duncan Bannatyne! Go on, be a little daring and venture outside your comfort zone – after all, it's only an exercise! If you prefer, you could play a variation of this exercise with friends, where each one of you has to come up with a fresh idea for each item. You could even award bonus points for those with the most innovative or unusual ideas. The trick is to get those creative juices flowing!

- **Supermarket food shop:** I buy mostly perishable organic fruit and vegetables. The trouble was that I couldn't resist a bargain! I would buy 'two for the price of one' or a bag of oranges instead of the couple that would actually get eaten during the week. Of course, much of it perished before the end of the week. It was like throwing money down the drain!

- **Books:** I was a sucker for a good book. Bookshops were my equivalent of sweet shops. I gradually became friends with my local library. I then started to let go of the books clogging up my home by lending them out to friends. If they came back, I reasoned that they were meant to stay with me.

- **Seminars:** Have you heard the expression 'seminar junkie'? Well, I'd like to think that I wasn't that bad. However, when I realised that I was going to workshops on how to write a book rather than actually writing a book, I knew something had to stop! I still go to workshops and retreats, as it's my favourite way to learn something and to meet like-minded people. However, now I set myself goals to complete first!

OK, so we've looked at the amount of money you are currently attracting, and at some of your beliefs about money. Remember, the two are linked. In Part 2 we'll look at transforming your old money beliefs so that you can start to attract more money.

Before we do that, though, let me ask you: 'Are you clear about how much money you really want?'

'Yes, of course I am!' I hear you exclaim. If so, write down the exact figure in the box below, and include the date when you will have this money.

> By ....(date), I expect to have £............ in my personal bank account.

- How did you reach that figure?
- Did you compare yourself with someone else?
- Did you simply pluck the figure out of 'thin air'?
- If you are truly expecting a certain amount, don't you think it may require a little more thought?
- What will that amount of money enable you to do with your life?
- How will it serve both you and others?
- How will it improve you as a person?

In Chapter 8 we look more closely at why it is important to have a clear vision of what you wish to achieve. At this point I am simply asking you to start considering how much and, most importantly, WHY?

■ *Case Study: Attracting an Exact Amount of Money*

Clara had just started her life-coaching business. She was renting a house and she longed to have enough money to get a mortgage for her own home.

Now self-employed, Clara realised that she'd be in a better position for a mortgage if she could show the bank six months' worth of regular income. Clara decided to attract exactly £1,200 a month for six months. Incredibly, at the end of each month, Clara's accounts showed she'd earned exactly £1,200.

Unfortunately, at the end of the six months her earnings dropped. Clara had achieved what she wanted, but she had forgotten to set a new financial goal!

Vision

Many people talk of attracting £10 million on the lottery. What would you do differently with £10 million?

A part of you knows that if you won the lottery tomorrow, you could relax and take life easy. The problem is that you weren't born on this earth to remain stagnant. We all yearn to grow and to become ALL that we can be. Sometimes the desire for money and security will push us to achieve much more than we initially think we can achieve. But then, what do we do once we've achieved it?

If we fully understand WHY we wish to achieve a certain amount of money and we feel that it is a deserving reason, we are more likely to attract the money we desire.

It's important to maintain a vision at all times. By keeping a vision of where we are going we will keep moving forward and growing. Be clear about what you want from the beginning and this book will help you get there.

I am constantly amazed by the number of people who tell me that they want to have more money. Yet when I ask them, 'how much money?' they have no answer. Sometimes they quickly grab a figure out of the air, maybe the amount announced on TV the night before or a number that reflects a friend's ambition and is no reflection of what they really want.

If you want something in your life, you need to be clear about what it is, whether it's money, winning a race or publishing a book in 30 different languages. That means investing time in your dreams and getting your vision clear. Remember, it is you and nobody else who creates your life … maybe it's time to start mastering your thoughts on the subject of 'Me and My Life'.

Checklist

- Why do you want to have more money?
- Do you want a regular stream of more money or one big windfall?

- Why?
- How will you change once you have more money in your pocket?
- Can you make that change without the money?
- Do you set yourself personal goals?
- Have you specific and time-related financial goals?
- What is your best idea for attracting more money?
- Have you taken action on it yet?
- Why not?

The money is already there. The only thing preventing you from being rich is you.

Part 2

Changing Habits

'We don't attract what we want,
we attract what we are.'
– Anonymous

The key steps to becoming a Money Magnet are in the
following chapters:

- breaking the pattern

- expecting money

- becoming rich

- clearing space

- following your passion

- taking action

- celebrating you!

They have been written in a certain order deliberately;
however, feel free to jump to a particular chapter if you
feel it is calling out to you.

4

Breaking the Pattern

> *'Unless you try to do something beyond what you have already mastered, you will never grow.'*
> – **Ralph Waldo Emerson**

Let's entertain the idea of you being rich.

In Part 1 you looked at how your thoughts create your reality. You explored the beliefs that you currently hold about money and about being wealthy. As many of your thoughts and beliefs are on an unconscious level, you then took some time to look at your current financial circumstances. By doing so, you gained an insight into how your thoughts have created your circumstances, and not the other way round.

Now it's time to change your mind about money. If you wish to change the results in your life, you need to change the thoughts that have created those results. By changing your thoughts about money, you can transform yourself into a Money Magnet!

A 'Money Magnet' is someone who always expects to receive an abundance of money and who enjoys an abundant life.

Are you ready to change your mind about money? Are you ready to let go of limiting beliefs and well-worn phrases? Are you prepared to behave differently around money?

It takes courage to change a life pattern. We live in a society of the quick, easy fix. We want to be transformed simply by reading a book. Many of the people who attend the 'How to Become a Money Magnet!' workshop receive an immediate increase in riches. However, they often then revert to their old thoughts and practices around money and, as a result, they soon return to their original financial position.

Your brain chooses the option with the least resistance. Your natural tendency is to stay in the 'comfort zone' that you've created for yourself. Thinking the same thoughts perpetuates a cycle in our lives.

So, to become a Money Magnet you need to adopt a different approach. To change your financial circumstances dramatically, you need to change your thoughts and your beliefs about money dramatically. You need to clear out the clutter of old, limiting thoughts to create space for new possibilities. You need to make your mind up about what you want!

The Power of Ceremony

One of the most powerful ingredients of the 'How to Become a Money Magnet!' workshop is the use of ceremony to release old beliefs and to set an intention for a new era of abundance. Sometimes this is all that is needed and the results can start to manifest within 24 hours of the workshop.

Ceremony works on both our conscious and unconscious thoughts, which is why it can be so effective in changing a pattern.

It can feel a little silly performing a ceremony, but that is the whole point. It can be an uncomfortable process and, as such, it pushes us beyond our normal comfort zone – it literally shifts our energetic vibration!

Performing a ceremony is like lifting a signpost up to the universe to announce the start of a new pattern. It can be very powerful.

■ *Case Study: Manifesting Gifts!*

'Marie-Claire, I am a Money Magnet! When I got home from the course, my mother rang me and said: "I think you need a new washing machine, I will buy you one for Christmas." I went and chose it yesterday and it arrives today.

'Later, my son was doing some photocopying and he said to me, "I am sorry, Mum, I have used your photocopier rather a lot. I had better buy you a new printer cartridge," and he gave me the money for a new one!'

– *Pat, North Wales*

What Makes Up a Ceremony?

The main ingredients of an effective ceremony are the use of intention and ritual.

Jan Cisek is a fellow Feng Shui consultant who specialises in 'branding', a particular type of Feng Shui that businesses (and individuals) use when they're thinking up logos and other ways to put forward their ideas and products and services. I remember attending one of his workshops where he described Feng Shui as 'intention plus energy plus ritual'. It's a great description that helps us to understand how we can transform energy, whether it's in our home, office, or even in our mind. You can shift your 'magnetic' pull through the power of intention and ritual.

In this chapter we look at changing our energy through ceremony or something outside of your usual behaviour patterns. In Chapter 5 we'll examine the power of intention.

> Feng Shui is intention plus energy plus ritual

Think of some of the ceremonies inherent in our culture and how powerful they can be in changing our lives. The ceremony of marriage can be so powerful that the connection remains very strong even in the case of divorce. For this reason, it can be a good idea to perform a type of ceremony to recognise divorce. Other ceremonies still practised in the UK include the very formal opening of Parliament and the changing of the guards.

Eating a family meal together at Christmas is a formal ceremony and in itself a celebration and recognition of our love for each other. Adopting the ceremony of a family meal on a regular basis can work wonders for love within a family. Such meals act as reminders, as statements, as corrections of the energy around each family member so that all feel realigned to the love among them.

Dating rituals are often discarded once a relationship is in full swing. Reserving one night a week, or a month, as your special 'date night' with your partner keeps alive the intention for a loving relationship.

Many of our culture's traditional ceremonies are dying out, and without ceremony we risk losing our focus on what is important.

This book is about money. I wonder if you already have any rituals with your money? For example, do you always pay all your bills on a particular day each month? Do you use a certain desk? When you go to see your bank manager, do you wear a well-chosen outfit and take the car rather than walk?

What Are My Rituals Around Money?

....

....

....

....

....

Do note that if you have no rituals around money, you may not be treating it with enough respect. Resolve today to build in some rituals to the way you handle your money. For example, schedule a regular time to do your bills each month or to check your expenditure and earnings sheets, and do these things in a way that makes you happy.

> If you are casual with money, it will be casual with you.

Enhancing Rituals with Intentions

We all use some ritual in our lives, from cleaning our teeth to washing the dishes. The trick is to enhance the power of a ritual by combining it with powerful thoughts.

For example, when paying your bills, take enough time to get comfortable at your favourite chair and desk. Maybe use your very special 'lucky' pen. Then take a few moments and a few deep breaths and reflect on your ability to pay these bills. Think of how fortunate you are to have attracted what money you have to pay the bills. Consider how lucky you are to have a roof over your head and food on your plate. Dwell a short while on all that you have for which you are grateful. Gratitude breeds more gratitude. You are celebrating your wealth every time you pay for something.

Money is simply energy. It is meant to flow from one person to another. Paying your bills keeps the flow going and creates space for new riches to come into your life. Enjoy paying your bills and enhance that enjoyment with the use of ceremony.

You can create your own ceremonies at home or in the office. Let me share with you some guidelines and examples that I have used over the years, to help you get a feel for the key elements involved.

Ceremony Guidelines

- Set aside plenty of time.

- Plan ahead so that you have everything you need to hand.

- Incorporate elements that are special to you, whether objects, poetry or specific movements.

- Have a clear intention about whether to clear or to attract something, or both, one after the other.

- Where possible, announce out loud your intention, ideally to witnesses.

- Be fully present, whether performing the ceremony or present as a witness.

- Incorporate elements that are outside your normal behaviour or environment.

The 'How to Become a Money Magnet!' Ceremony

Inevitably, a ceremony is considerably enhanced when it is witnessed by several people. There is good reason why wedding ceremonies normally include witnesses. If we make a statement to ourselves, it will have less power than if we share our statement with another, and even more power if we share our wishes with our family, our friends or any other supportive group.

Each 'How to Become a Money Magnet!' workshop ceremony is created by the people in the room at the time, each person contributing an idea or an action for the whole group.

Typical contributions include solemnly lighting a candle for each person, providing a shoulder massage for each participant, reading out a poem or creating a flower arrangement. We adapt the ceremony to the season, so that in summer we often walk over to some nearby woods and use the river in our ceremony.

At the core of the ceremony is the opportunity for each person to declare solemnly to the group that he or she is now letting go of old, inhibiting money beliefs such as 'I'm not good enough to receive.' The person will then symbolically dispose of this old belief. Ways of doing this have included ceremoniously placing a written copy of the old belief into a fire or into a river stream to be washed away. Feel free to be creative with how you wish to do this.

■ Case Study: Burning Our Limiting Beliefs

I remember attending a residential workshop with Diana Cooper where we created paper 'coffins' to contain our old beliefs. These were either written down on a piece of paper or represented by an object. Then, in formal dress and with great ceremony, we placed them in the fire while announcing to all present that we had let go of our limiting belief.

At the time I was a chain smoker, and so my 'coffin' contained my cigarettes. I am happy to announce that I am now free of what was a 20-year-old habit.

During the summer Money Magnet workshops, we write our limiting beliefs on short pieces of wood or on paper wrapped around wood. We throw them ceremoniously into a fast-moving stream, often with cows as our audience! There was one occasion when there were bullocks in the field. This added an extra element of fear, and therefore courage, to the proceedings!

Space Clearing

As a Feng Shui consultant I use the ceremony of 'space clearing' to help shift old beliefs and stagnant situations. Space clearing is a way of shifting the energy in a room or home or even office. It is traditionally done using Native American sage.

Lighting the sage, in the form of a 'smudge stick', you waft the smoky aroma through the space, all the time maintaining your intention to clear all negative or limiting energy.

■ *Case Study: Space Clearing*

Paul and Rita called me in because they were suffering with health, wealth and relationship problems. Paul's headaches were making him irritable and, weighed down with money issues, their relationship was suffering.

Following a thorough space-clearing of their whole home, Rita called me two days later. 'I can't believe it, Marie-Claire! Paul's headaches have gone and he is like a new man. He even ironed two baskets of washing for the first time in 10 years! Our relationship is much more loving: where we used to turn our backs in bed, we now hold hands and cuddle up.'

A week later Rita called me again to say that Paul had just won an all-expenses paid one-week opportunity to work in Mauritius!

Interestingly, it was Paul who had been in the house while I'd performed the space-clearing, even agreeing to turn off his precious cricket during the ceremony! And it was Paul who had received the maximum benefit.

'Poor Me!' Becomes 'Lucky Me!'

As I have already mentioned, attracting money is easy. If we haven't enough money in our lives, it is evidence that we are not thinking 'wealthy' thoughts.

Fortunately I realised this early on in my career and, using what I knew, I was able to achieve considerable financial success in my career.

However, as I've also mentioned, some years ago I made a mistake and invested in a house with someone who was inherently unreliable. He stripped the house of everything and then vanished. I was left with a house worth substantially less than I had invested, and I descended into the depths of 'poor me'.

I stopped working for three months and invested all my cash savings to put the property back together again. As I painted the walls myself, I reinforced the 'martyr' thinking of 'poor me'. The more I thought 'poor me', the more money seemed to pour out of my bank account into this house. When I realised that with no money left I was going to have to move into the house, I knew that I needed to create a dramatic shift in the energy!

The day that the carpets were due to be laid, I arrived at the house very early in the morning. My intention was to let go of the 'poor me' and to welcome in a new era of abundance. I needed a ceremony that was radical for me and totally different to anything I had previously done. I needed a drastic shift in my energy and in my belief systems!

Taking one of the leftover tins of white paint, I started painting the wooden staircase steps where the carpet was to be laid. On the first step went the word 'welcome'. On the second step the word 'joy', and the third step 'peace'. I carried on, painting a different word on each step, finishing with 'abundance' which literally seemed to 'dance' into the bathroom.

Then I started on the wooden floorboards of the landing with 'thank you'. Having spent months berating the lack of help with the house, I now painted the floor with the name of each person who had helped me with the home, even starting with the name of my unreliable partner, without whom I wouldn't have had the home in the first place. I continued to paint love and inspiration symbols in one bedroom, and money signs in the second bedroom. When I was finished painting, I danced around the house singing out loud the words I had written. And as I sang, I felt a shift in how I felt about the house and about my circumstances.

The results were immediate – and I think I may have shifted my beliefs about men as well as about money! An ex-boyfriend appeared that day and took me to lunch. He was unusually amorous! Then a gas man arrived to do a job on the house and asked me out. Then the carpet men arrived and offered me the most expensive underlay for free.

I soon realised that far from being in a nightmare situation, thanks to my original decision I was now lucky enough to be living rent-free and mortgage-free! The effort and money that I'd used meant that I was not only living mortgage-free but I had a brand new bathroom and kitchen and a wonderful new layout to my home! Wasn't I the lucky one?

Using the power of ceremony, I had shifted from 'poor me' to 'lucky me'. If you don't like the results that you are manifesting in your life, be honest about your thought patterns and do something radical to shift them!

Doing Something Out of the Ordinary

Maybe ceremony just isn't your thing. It all sounds just a little too wacky for you.

If this is the case, then instead I recommend that you find a way to do something NEW, something different, something that's a change from your normal routine or way of doing things. When you do something outside of your normal patterns it serves as a wake-up call to your energetic pattern and can open up a chance for change.

Anything that takes you out of your comfort zone is good, whether it is walking on hot coals or actually paying your bills on time!

> 'If you always do what you've always done, you'll always get what you've always gotten.'
> – *Anthony Robbins*

Of course, it's not comfortable to step outside our comfort zone. Instead, many of us settle into our nests of 'affordability'. We persuade ourselves that we're OK as we are, that we can get by, even if we haven't got as much money as we'd like.

Sooner or later, however, the level of buried dissatisfaction will reach breaking point and we'll feel we simply have to do something about our situation. It's a bit like the alcoholic who will ignore his drinking problem for as long as he can, but sooner or later the 'nest' becomes intolerable and he is finally ready to risk jumping out. In jumping out, in doing something totally different to all previous behaviour, he just may learn to fly.

> What is it that you are not doing, and that you know you could do, to improve your financial situation, right now?

And so it is with money.

- If you've always been employed, why not consider becoming self-employed?

- If you're self-employed, why not collaborate and think bigger solutions?

- If you've always wanted to be a published author, why not start writing?

- If you've always wanted to have the home of your dreams, why not start saving?

- If you've never had enough money, why not invest in changing your beliefs about money?

- If you're full of great ideas but never seem to get started on them, use a coach to help you with the process of turning each idea into reality.

> Next time your heart jumps for joy, honour its desire.

■ *Case Study: Investing in a Coach*

Sharon was a self-employed mother of two who had remortgaged and now found herself in considerable debt. Her newly created business wasn't going well. Every time things looked hopeful, something came along to dash her hopes. Sharon's turning point came when she heard me give a talk to WiRE (Women in Rural Enterprise) and she realised that the only barrier to her success was herself.

Sharon then did something that was out of the ordinary for her. Despite having very little disposable income, she invested both time and money in three months of my coaching, taking a 40-minute train journey to get to the appointments.

By doing something out of the ordinary and that required effort, Sharon was then able to access and clear her limiting beliefs about money, some of which stemmed from a lack of self-worth, reinforced since the age of five.

Now Sharon has rediscovered her sense of worth, she is facing up to her responsibilities and attracting lucrative opportunities to create a healthy income for herself and her family's future. And she is happy.

Commit today to doing something outside of your ordinary pattern.

Checklist

- Who is responsible for your current financial situation?

- How can you think differently about your current financial situation?

- What can you do differently?

- How can you mark the start of a new era of abundance?

- What have you been putting off that you know needs doing?

- How often do you find yourself thinking 'poor me'?

- How can you change those thoughts?

- What is the one thing that you know you could do but that you are scared of doing?

- Can you imagine being successful at it?

The money is already there.
The only thing preventing you from being rich is you.

5

Expecting More Money

> *'Our intention creates our reality.'*
> **– Wayne Dyer**

Now you are committed to improving your money situation – Congratulations! You have taken the first step by deciding to read this book and by following the previous chapter's instruction to do something different.

How did you let go of that old belief that you were just not good enough? Did you light a candle with a friend and burn a piece of paper with it written on? Did you use the power of ceremony or did you do something that you've never done before? Did you get out all your bills and receipts to discover your exact financial position? Did you commit to a new savings plan? Remember, we have to change our patterns if we wish to enjoy a different outcome.

Exercise

If you haven't yet done something different, take a moment now and write down the one thing that you will do now to start to change your approach to money:

....
....
....
....

The Power of Intention

Too many people exclaim, 'Oh I want to have more money!' without ever getting specific. Without any clear intention, such a comment is but a wish, at best. At worst, the statement might as well be, 'If only I had more money!' This is the same as saying 'I'll never have more than I have now.' While the conscious words may state a request or even an intention for money, the unconscious intention is to remain with the status quo.

To shift this state of paralysis, we need to get specific and we need to include a time frame.

> Have you ever noticed that when you have limited time to do something, it actually takes you less time to do it?

Similarly, by setting a time limit and being clear on when you will have this money, it will become easier to manifest it.

Exercise: Stretching the Possibilities

How much would you like in your bank account?

Now multiply that figure by 10 and imagine receiving that amount of money.

How does it feel?

Does it feel uncomfortable? (It can be too big a leap for most people.)

Now think back to your original sum and double it.

Odds are that the new higher figure doesn't feel too uncomfortable now, even though only minutes earlier half that figure was the maximum that you could imagine receiving.

Once the mind is stretched, it cannot go back to its original state.

Whatever it is that you want, however much money you would like to have in your bank accounts, sooner or later the next step is to *set an intention*.

In other words, you reach a moment of decision. You get clear on exactly what you want and you decide to attract it, usually by a certain date. In setting an intention, you commit to it happening. You shift from a position of 'maybe it will happen' to 'I know that it can happen.' Having a clear expectation of what you truly desire is a key step in the process of becoming a Money Magnet.

■ Case Study: Setting an Intention

Peter was wedded to his job. He had become a workaholic, working evenings and weekends. It was finally too much for him and Peter decided to leave his job. He also decided to get the security of a decent pay-off when he left.

I asked him to picture the sum of money he wanted. Then I asked him to double it. I repeatedly asked him to double the amount he envisioned until we reached his maximum comfort level. (We often aim far too low in our expectations.)

Keeping a clear expectation of this amount of money, Peter resigned.

He officially left work a few weeks later with the exact amount of money that he had envisaged. In fact, he was so successful that he was delighted to pay the £100,000 tax bill!

This newly attracted money enabled Peter to take the time out he needed to de-stress, to do some travelling and to decide what he really wanted from life.

Using Clear Intentions to Achieve Sales Targets

Whenever we have a clear intention, we make it easier for the 'universe' to assist us. I learned this technique from my earlier years as a sales manager. Rewarded with exciting incentives, there was always enough motivation to achieve the set target of sales per month.

The trick is to EXPECT it, even when the evidence may be saying otherwise!

Often with a monthly sales target of over £1 million revenue, my sales team would achieve it in the very last few minutes of the month! They were exciting times, and as long as we stayed 100 per cent focused on achieving the target, we achieved it.

Acting 'As If'

I remember that at every half-year point, I rewarded the team with a day trip to the sea where we would spend the day on boats and jet-skis. As we neared the June deadline, you could hear the team describing to each other what fun they were going to be having at the end of the month and whether they were going to choose the sailing boat or the jet-ski. In other words, they were already *expecting* to exceed the mid-year sales target. And I don't remember one year when we didn't achieve those sales targets.

Similarly, when we were promised bonuses for exceptional sales performance, I would often spend my bonus money before I actually received it. Quite simply, I expected to receive it, so I acted as though I had actually been guaranteed it. The intention was clearly set for me to receive that exact amount. I behaved as though it was already 'in the bag' – and I always did receive it. Always.

What are you expecting to receive financially over the next month?

Would you like to set a new intention?

> Set an intention for what you really want, NOT for what you think you'll be able to achieve.

We often feel limited by outside constraints:

'Oh, my firm would never pay me money if I decided to leave my job.'

'Nobody's ever earned that much in this job.'

'I'm just not that lucky.'

Watch out for comments like these and discard them the moment you become aware of them. Start believing in miracles. Start small if need be, but start to push the boundaries of what you think may be possible. Remember: set an intention for what you really want, not for what you think you'll be able to achieve. There's a big difference between the two.

■ Case Study: Setting an Intention and Letting Go of the 'How'

At work I was responsible for more than 80 per cent of the company's sales, and though I always achieved my targets and was well paid, I'd become bored with the job and, in my heart, I knew that I was ready to move on.

The problem was saying 'no' to a comfortable salary and all the perks that came with it. I decided that I'd feel a lot happier leaving work if I could leave with an extra bonus.

Leaving for a two-week holiday, I discreetly cleared my office of all my personal items, acting as if I would not be returning after the holiday. During the holiday itself, I became clearer and clearer that I would not be returning to work, and the figure of £30,000 became ingrained in my mind. I had no idea HOW I would actually leave the job, as I still couldn't actually see myself resigning. But I kept the intention of leaving work and the figure of £30,000 in my mind.

On the night of my return, my boss called to ask if I could meet him at a café before coming to the office next day. I remember feeling delighted and telling my sister that I would be back within the hour. After sharing my future plans with my boss, he actually agreed with me that my dream of doing even more travelling was what was right for me just then. I said 'I can't afford to leave the job, though,' to which he replied, 'How much would you need?' I was taken aback, but answered, 'Well, about £30,000.' To my astonishment, he answered, 'Well, OK, for the person who has been responsible for over 80 per cent of the company's business, I'd say that's fair enough!' Within the hour I'd left my job with a promise of over £30,000 coming my way. I only ever went back to the office for my leaving do!

The above story is not the only time that I have managed to leave a job in a way that suited me best. Previously working for a 'jobs for life' corporation, I set my intention to leave for a more lucrative industry.

Having worked for the company for more than 10 years, rightly or wrongly I expected a certain sum of money for my efforts. Staying focused and clear on my goal, I left voluntarily with a lump sum in my pocket. I started my new job two weeks later.

It doesn't matter whether what you want has been achieved beforehand. All that matters is that you are clear on what you want. It's good to have a timescale and a good reason why you want what you want. Then it is simply a question of taking one step after another as they present themselves.

■ Case Study: Intention Releases Available Funds

Joanna decided to redecorate her main bedroom. Her intention was clear and she went ahead and started to clear the room in anticipation. The fact that Joanna didn't have any spare money to pay for the redecoration did not deter her from her objective. She didn't allow her circumstances to influence her thoughts. She expected to accomplish the task.

Imagine Joanna's satisfaction when, on clearing the bedroom, she came across £400 cash on top of the wardrobe. It was the perfect amount to pay for her bedroom's redecoration!

Is it a coincidence that we find the money just when we need it? What about all those times when we don't find money?

If you set a clear enough intention and you truly expect the result, then you will always find the money. The trick, of course, is to manage your thoughts. You need thoughts of anticipation rather than hope. You need thoughts of expectation rather than desire.

You Can Expect More Money ...

How can you suddenly start expecting more money if the external evidence suggests otherwise? Recapping on what we have covered so far, you can expect more money because you have:

- read and digested this book

- performed a ceremony to mark the start of a new way of thinking about money

- become responsible for your finances by checking your accounts

- let go of 'how' it will happen

- had a clear intention to attract a certain amount

- done something different to attract more money

- behaved 'as if' you expect more money

- done whatever needs doing to help you to expect more money!

You know better than anyone what you need to do, now.

■ *Case Study: Expecting Money from a Certain Source*

My friend Molly, a training consultant, wished to be employed by one of the major banks.

Molly stated her intention by writing herself a cheque from the bank in question for £200,000. She dated the cheque and pinned it on her noticeboard.

Two years later she realised that she had, in fact, attracted a total sum of £200,000 earnings from this particular bank over the previous two years. Looking at her noticeboard, Molly noticed that the cheque was dated for that year.

Changing Your Thoughts by Changing What You See

Your subconscious mind sees what it sees. What it sees influences the subconscious thought, which then endeavours to create the reality of what it sees. In the above example Molly's subconscious mind saw the cheque and so expected it to be real. Her thoughts then set about creating that reality.

Exercise

What are you looking at every day? Does it reflect the reality that you desire? How can you improve things?

....

....

....

....

....

As a Feng Shui consultant, I advise people on how their surroundings can support their desires. I am often called in when life is not running smoothly, and I'll find the clues on the walls in the home.

■ *Case Study: Art of Influence*

Hannah and her husband were marketing consultants who had moved from Leeds to London 10 months earlier. Unfortunately, they hadn't been able to sell their beautiful five-bedroomed home in Leeds. This meant they had the considerable expense of running two homes, and money seemed to be trickling away from Hannah and her husband.

When I visited the home in Leeds, I discovered a collection of old pictures lacking any colour and featuring images of people weighed down by the burden of extreme poverty. They were very depressing.

Needless to say, I recommended their immediate removal, and the fortunes of Hannah and her husband improved. The house was sold and they were able to enjoy their new life in London.

Vision Boards

Why not collect images of how your life would look with more money? Collect images of experiences that make you smile and that you would like to attract into your life. Arrange them attractively on a board or in a picture frame so that you can glance at them every day. Then you can simply leave it to your subconscious to work out a way to attract those specific things, giving you a 'nudge' along the way when you need to do something different.

In the film *The Secret*, we see James Ray moving into a spectacular new house. Among the boxes being unpacked, his son discovers James' old vision boards. On one of the vision boards, made some years earlier, is a picture of the exact house that has just become their new home.

Create yourself a vision board and get yourself into a position where you expect riches!

■ *Case Study: Vision Boards Do Work!*

Mitch in Canada is an agent for aspiring authors. He keeps a vision board in his office, where he collects pictures of everything that he wishes to experience in his life. On it were pictures of the

Bahamas, the Cayman Islands and Jamaica. He also had the name of a specific cruise liner.

One day he received a call from his client and friend, Peggy, inviting him to join her on a cruise. Have you guessed?

The cruise ship was visiting the exact destinations featured on Mitch's vision board! It even turned out to be the exact cruise company that was featured on Mitch's vision board!

Of course, one of the best ways to influence your thoughts is through the language you use. This brings us neatly to the next chapter, and how you can change your language to attract more money.

Checklist

- Are you clear on what you want?

- Are the images in your home and office supporting your dreams?

- Have you set a clear intention of what you want to achieve by a certain date?

- Are you confident that you can achieve it irrespective of external circumstances and others' opinions?

- How are you going to maintain your faith?

- Have you developed an inner 'knowing' that it is possible?

- Are you willing to trust your intuition and act on any opportunities presented to you?

The money is already there. The only thing preventing you from being rich is you.

6

Becoming Rich

'Whatever it is you are feeling, is a perfect reflection of what is in the process of becoming.'
– Esther Hicks

Listening to the language you use, whether on paper, in speech or in the way you think, can help you to become a Money Magnet. Your mind, body and spirit are intrinsically linked. In choosing your words carefully, you can choose to feel more positive. Your positive feelings will then act as a magnet, attracting more reasons to feel positive. In this chapter we will explore how you can use your words and feelings to become more attractive to money. We will look at how important it is to 'be' wealthy, in order that wealth comes to you.

Riches are coming your way. Be as you would be if you knew that you were due to come into some money. No doubt you would feel happier with life and less stressed. Imagine for a moment ... that you wake up tomorrow morning to open a letter in the post ... and the letter announces that you are receiving an unexpected win of £10 million.

PAUSE to really feel what this feels like.

Are you smiling?

Or maybe laughing hysterically?

Has your body relaxed?

Can you feel joy in your bones?

How does it feel to be rich?

Get into the feeling. It feels good, doesn't it?

See how long you can continue feeling 'as if' you are now rich.

A friend calls you. Do you tell her your news or do you simply smile inwardly?

Are you different in the way you respond to her?

How are you different?

People who know that they have enough money behave differently to those who worry about where the next penny is coming from.

They will think differently, behave differently and speak differently.

They may hold themselves more confidently.

They may have more time to listen to others.

They may have more confidence in taking occasional risks.

They may trust their judgement more easily than those with less money do.

Exercise

List some ways in which a wealthy person behaves differently to a person with less money

....

....

....

....

....

In Chapter 1 you discovered that everything is made up of energy, and that the difference between one thing and another is a difference of vibration. We are like magnets attracting similar vibrations. 'Like attracts like' and 'what goes round, comes round' are common expressions in our language. Your thoughts, feelings, language and actions are all at a certain vibration level. In order to become a Money Magnet, you need to think, feel, speak and act as though you already are a Money Magnet. It is simple.

'No, not that simple,' I hear you exclaim. 'If it were that simple, wouldn't we all be rich by now?'

The answer is: yes; yes it is simple, and yes we can all be rich. In fact, we were born to be rich. In this chapter we'll look at what you can do to start feeling rich straight away. In the next chapter we'll clear up any blocks that are getting in your way.

Before you look at changing your vibration, let's take a very brief moment to look at how you *don't* wish to be.

The 'Poor Me' Vibe

How would you feel, speak and act if you felt that you didn't have enough money?

Did you try to get hold of this book at a discount or even for free by borrowing it from the library or a friend?

Do you always take the cheapest quote or do you shop around for the best service?

Are you ever resentful or jealous of another's success?

How often do you complain about life being unfair?

Are you surrounded by friends who boast about the bargains they find?

Have you ever been accused of being a cheapskate?

I remember a friend of mine telling me that she always had the impression that I wanted things for free. I was quite upset that she should think that of me. It was precisely what I advised people *not* to do. Then I took some time to be honest with myself and I realised that, yes, there is a part of me that absolutely loves a bargain.

Exercise

List all the ways in which a person with less money behaves differently to a person with plenty of money

....

....

....

....

....

....

Do you recognise any of your own behaviour in the above list?

Be courageously honest.

It is time to acknowledge how you are attracting a life with less fortune, simply in the way that you are behaving (or vibrating, to be exact).

Let me share an example.

My friend Stevie and I decided to go on Bob Proctor's Caribbean cruise. This would be a great week of learning from seminars and connecting with like-minded people. The cheapest cabins were £800 for the week. However, neither of us wanted to stay in a cabin with no sea view or balcony. So we set an intention to pay only £800 for an upgraded cabin and, because we expected it, that's what we received (see previous chapter!).

We were naturally thrilled with our mastery of the situation ... that is, until we started talking to other guests on the ship! We then realised that some of them had paid even less money for their cabins! Now we weren't feeling quite so happy, or masterful, or rich. Now we were starting to let feelings of resentment creep in.

The cruise included talks from a number of motivational speakers, and one day we heard the speaker Paul Martinelli share his secrets for success. One secret in particular stood out: 'Accept the Going Price.'

His principle was that when you want something, you value it and you are happy to pay for it: simple. That's how a wealthy person would behave. What a waste of energy to haggle when you could be using your energy more productively. What a contradiction to want something and then to discount its value by trying to get it at a lower price. And in understanding this truth, our energies shifted back to a higher vibration.

Within the next hour I overheard a woman sharing how she had been upgraded to VIP status as a result of paying more for her cabin than others had paid. It didn't take me long to act on what I had learned. Imagine my delight in announcing to Stevie that we had now been upgraded to VIP status. VIP status included a gift worth $2,000 and private morning sessions with Bob Proctor!

As soon as we shifted our approach to the situation, we then attracted the better situation. Easy!

Let's look at your scenario.

What is it in your life that you wish to improve?

What are you thinking about your current financial circumstances?

How can you change the way you are currently thinking about the situation?

Often when we dwell on a negative statement, it leads to another, and another. It snowballs until things are really bad. If we share our bad news with a friend, we double the negative energy that we're devoting to it (unless you choose that friend very carefully!).

If you don't like your job or the person you answer to at work, for example, don't focus all your energies on why things are not good. Instead, look for the positives. Then you will no longer be a match for the negative vibration, and either the job will change or the other person will change. Instead of 'poor me', you take on the very different mantle of 'lucky me!'

Exercise

Write down at least three negative statements about your current situation. Then cross them out and replace them with a positive version of each statement.

For example: 'I can't afford to buy that book I really wanted' is crossed out to become 'I'm so lucky to live in a country with free access to library books whenever I wish.'

....

....

....

....

....

....

The crossing out of the negative statement is important. It signals to your subconscious that the negative statement is no longer valid.

Changing the pattern of your thoughts takes practice. You have to be totally committed to manifesting a better life for yourself. And I've found that it helps to have a coach or a good friend who will keep you on track.

One day I met my mother in town for a coffee. She knew that a couple of years earlier I'd felt that I'd made a very poor investment decision. My bad habit was to complain about the situation. My mother had cut out some text from a magazine and pasted it onto the back of one of my late father's business cards. These were the words:

> 'It's pointless to have regrets. If you took a decision for a good reason at the time, that was the best you could do so there's no point regretting it.'

It stopped me in my tracks and it helped me to stop my negative thinking. We all need a friend or a coach to point us in the right direction every now and again.

Start the Day with Happy Thoughts

Start the day, while still in bed, with some happy, grateful thoughts. Focus on one of your goals and imagine for a few moments that you have already achieved that goal. Feel what it feels like in every cell of your body. Enjoy the happy sensation as much as you can.

Greet yourself in the mirror with a big smile. Check your thoughts while in the shower and getting dressed. If a negative thought sneaks in, acknowledge it and let it go. Get curious about how you can find positives where before you only found negatives. This can be particularly effective when your negative thoughts are about another person. As you think positively about him or her, that person is far more likely to meet your positive expectations.

▪ Case Study: Positive Thought, Positive Relationships

I was having negative thoughts about how little my partner did around the house. These thoughts were definitely sapping my energy levels. So I set about finding positive things to think about him. This was difficult at first.

When we judge someone else for their faults, we often do it as a shortcut to feeling better about ourselves. As such, it can seem like a good idea at the time. I promise you, though, that it will simply reinforce the thing you are complaining about.

Once I realised what I was doing, the next morning I found a way to think more positively about my partner and his contribution to the house. That very evening, with no word from me, he returned from work and immediately went to work cleaning the oven and then the shower! It was indeed a miracle, and evidence yet again as to the power of our thoughts.

Why not try it at home with your partner or friend? Do email me to let me know how you get on! (mc@ marieclairecarlyle.com)

You can apply the same principles in a work situation. Simply by changing your thoughts about the situation at work, you can improve it. Incidentally, if you are planning to ask your bosses for a pay rise, make sure you are absolutely convinced within yourself that they will say 'Yes' before you ask. If need be, spend some time justifying it to yourself by writing out reasons for your pay rise beforehand. Do whatever you need to do to convince yourself that you deserve a pay rise, and only when you are 100 per cent convinced, ask your boss. Asking for anything when you expect 'No' for an answer is, at the very least, a waste of breath. At its worst, it is creating another reason for you to feel unworthy and a victim of your circumstances.

> You can take control of your life and your finances by taking control of your thoughts, now.

■ *Case Study: Improving Your Reality with Your Mind*

I was working for a boss who had a very intimidating manner. Nothing ever seemed good enough for him. He'd bark orders at us and rarely showed any interest in or had any praise for his staff. It had got to the point where I dreaded working alongside him and I frequently felt close to tears.

Finally I *decided* to do something about the situation. I decided to think positive thoughts about my boss. Sometimes this is easier said than done, especially when you've invested a lot of energy in feeling bad towards someone.

In the end I managed to think better thoughts about him by 'putting myself in his shoes': I felt what it was like to have the stress of running my own business, of being recently divorced, of losing my family home of 22 years and of not being able to give up smoking. It was easier then to feel some compassion towards him.

The next Monday morning, he was like a completely different person. He asked about my weekend, he made me breakfast, he was polite and considerate. In fact, when he asked me out for lunch, I actually thought that I might have gone too far!

My job became much less stressful, and when shortly afterwards I found an even better position and decided to move on, my boss and I parted on amicable terms.

When you judge a situation as bad and you focus on the bad, you start to unpick all that you may have once liked about it. As you pick away, you start to unravel all that is good and positive about a person or a situation until all you can see is 'poor me ... how have I ended up in this bad situation?'

If you want to change your situation, start changing your thoughts about it NOW!

Affirmations

A relatively easy way to help you change how you think and feel about your situation is to change what you *say* about your situation. This is where the use of affirmations can be helpful. An affirmation is a simple positive statement that is repeated on a regular basis until the mind adopts it as a new belief. Some people like to keep copies of their favourite affirmations in places where they can see them regularly, for example inside a kitchen cupboard or written in secret code on the steering wheel of their car.

Examples of affirmations for becoming a Money Magnet include the following:

I am (now) a Money Magnet!

I'm always finding money.

I attract money wherever I go.

I am happy, healthy and wealthy.

I love my life.

I have all that I need and more.

I deserve lots of money.

I love money and all that it allows me to do.

I respect money and money respects me.

I make money easily.

I value what I do.

I offer enormous value.

I am happy to receive my full worth.

Exercise: My Favourite Affirmations

Write down the affirmations that feel most comfortable for you:

....

....

....

....

....

Self-worth

> *'There is no amount of money in the world that will make you comfortable if you are not comfortable with yourself.'* – Stuart Wilde

The link between your feelings of self-worth and being a Money Magnet is so essential that it is worth looking at again. You may be holding back your natural flow of abundance through a lack of self-worth.

Looking back, I've enjoyed periods in my life when I've attracted huge amounts of money and success ... and then I've done something to sabotage it. It was as though there was a limit to how happy I was 'allowed' to be. The up-and-down cycle of my wealth was an indicator of how worthy I felt as an individual. Once I understood this, it was much easier to do something about it, using many of the techniques in this book.

Find an affirmation that starts to build your self-confidence. My personal favourite is 'I'm OK just as I am.' It just seems to roll off my tongue without trying too hard, and I can noticeably feel my body relaxing when I say or think it.

Exercise

My personal affirmation to increase my self-worth is:

....

....

To create your own affirmations, follow these simple guidelines – and have fun putting together words that, when used often enough, can literally transform your life!

Exercise: Create Your Own Affirmations

Follow these guidelines:

Keep it personal, using 'I' where it's natural to do so.

Keep it simple.

Keep it natural and something that you would find easy to say often.

Create a rhyme or rhythm to it.

Keep it positive ('I'm giving up being broke' is negative).

Keep it credible.

Keep it in your natural language.

Keeping It Credible

If you are saying 'I am wealthy' as an affirmation and yet, every time you say it, you have a little voice in your head exclaiming, 'Yeah, right! Have you seen your bank balance lately?' then it will not be a very effective affirmation! In fact it could even have the opposite effect to the one desired. An alternative affirmation might be, 'I'm ready to receive more wealth into my life.' As things start to improve, you may then adjust your affirmation to 'I'm starting to attract more money.' This may become 'I am a Money Magnet!' which may then lead to 'I am wealthy!'

Participants who've completed the 'How to Become a Money Magnet!' course are able to say, 'I am a Money Magnet!' The fact that they have been on the course is evidence in itself that this is now a credible statement. In the same way, once you have read and inwardly digested this book and completed the exercises, you too will be able to affirm, 'I am a Money Magnet!'

■ Case Study: The Power of Thought

Whenever I have a stand at a fair, I stop passers-by with a bowl of affirmations. 'Help yourself to a free affirmation,' I invite them. 'Each one is different, so you will pick the one that you need the most.'

Why does one person pick up one card and another person select a different one? Nothing happens by accident, and my intention is that each person picks up the card that he or she most needs. As people select their card, the odds are that they too are hoping with their thoughts that they will pick the one card that will make the biggest difference to their life. And, time after time, I have watched as people select an affirmation that is the complete opposite of their most overriding negative thought.

For example, a woman selects 'I am wealthy' and she immediately exclaims, 'Have you seen my bills?'

An attractive 16-year-old selects 'I am beautiful' only to shrivel her face up in disgust and tell me that she can't even bear to look in the mirror.

One of my favourites is the affirmation 'Life is Easy!' simply because of the reactions it causes. People are so used to complaining about how hard life is (a message that is consistently reinforced through the media) that the idea that 'life is easy' literally stops them in their tracks!

What affirmation would make the biggest difference to your life?

Write it down and start using it NOW.

The Be-Do-Have Principle

Are you waiting to have money in the bank before you do the thing you've always wanted to do and be as happy as you can be?

Are you miserable in your job but waiting until things are better financially before you leave?

Have you always wanted to write a book but are waiting until you have enough time?

Are you waiting until you're rich to be happy?

If you can relate to the above comments and you are waiting to have something before you can be happy, you have got it the wrong way round! Maybe that's why you haven't progressed as much as you'd like. Maybe that's why you feel 'true happiness' is avoiding you.

The principle of Be-Do-Have is that you have to *be* the person you want to be first, in order to then *do* as that person would do, in order to then *have* all that you want to have.

If you start to behave as a lucky person, for example, you will start to attract luck wherever you go. You become a magnet for good fortune. You may then have the confidence to take decisions that you may not have made before you considered yourself lucky, and you will attract things into your life that you've always wanted.

Rather than waiting until you are wealthier, you can decide to be happy and wealthy right now. Today, you can be happy if you really want to be happy. Look around for something that is good about you or your life. Look to nature and find something beautiful that will make you smile. Think of the last time you were laughing and feel that joy inside again. By choosing to be happy now, you will attract things to do and to have that make you happy. Remember, it's all in the vibes that you're giving out. Be a magnet for happiness and you will be a magnet for money.

If you wish to be a Money Magnet, start emitting the vibes of someone who has money. Be generous from the heart and you will naturally attract more money. Be grateful for all the amazing abundance that you already have in your life: your health, your sight, your loved ones. Behave like someone who is confident in their ability to make money, and you will attract the opportunities to make it. Bemoan your situation and the opportunities will do a U-turn at the end of your street.

Be rich in your dealings with others and you will become rich in what you have in your life. It's the Be-Do-Have Principle! Resolve to apply it in your life now!

Exercise

How are you going to 'be-have' differently in order to attract more money into your life?

....

....

....

....

■ *Case Study: The Be-Do-Have Principle*

I yearned to drive my own convertible sports car. The problem was that I was a salesperson, and salespeople just didn't get company cars that were convertibles.

I wasn't selling so much that I could buy my own car for the weekends.

Instead of focusing on the fact that I didn't have a convertible, I found a way to be a convertible driver by borrowing my friend's convertible whenever I could.

Soon afterwards, I got a break at work. I was offered the opportunity to do the Management Training Programme. In due course I became a Manager, and I could now have my own convertible company car.

Note that instead of waiting to be happy driving my own convertible, I chose a way to experience being happy driving a convertible, and then I attracted a way to have the car.

Pining for what you want doesn't work. Start being who you really want to be and you will attract what you need to do, to have all that you want to have.

Checklist

- If you'd like a new car, book it for a test drive today.

- If you'd like to be fitter, start training regularly like an athlete.

- If you'd like to live in a castle, book a weekend away in one.

- If you'd like to have more money, be more generous in your daily dealings.

The money is already there.
The only thing preventing you from being rich is you.

Part 3

Exploring Your Potential

'And the day came when the risk to remain tight in a bud was more painful than the risk it took to blossom.'

– Anaïs Nin

7

Clearing Space

*'When the magnet does not attract the needle,
the fault lies in the dirt that covers up the
needle.'*

– Sri Safya Sai Baba

In Feng Shui we look at the energy of a home and how
it flows from room to room. When there is clutter in
the home, it slows down the energy. Have you noticed
how someone with a lot of clutter in his home is often
tired and never seems to have enough money?

Money is energy. If you wish to have more money, you
need to create space for new energy. That space may be
in your home or your office. It may be in your schedule.
It may be in your thoughts. Let's look at them all.

For many people, clearing their clutter is the turning
point towards becoming a Money Magnet.

> Clutter is the stuff in our homes and in our heads
> that gets in the way of living the life we desire.

■ *Case Study: From Clutter to Riches*

When I first arrived at the house, I thought I was at the wrong address. Through the window, all I could make out were boxes piled up high and a room full of disarray. It looked more like a squat than the home of a young entrepreneur! That's when Chantal appeared at the door.

Chantal is the owner of four radio stations, yet she had called me because she had no money. The last straw was when her bicycle was stolen. She couldn't afford a new one. On entering her home I was to discover that Chantal and her partner had been living in only half of their home for the past five years. The rest of the house was piled high with clutter.

During the course of our consultation, we established the reason for the clutter – and then performed a ceremonious space-clearing. Chantal cleared a total of seven car-loads of clutter that very day. Within a month Chantal had her home back, and celebrated with a drinks party in the cleared rooms!

Within six months Chantal's financial situation had been completely transformed. Sales in her business had doubled. She had been able to buy herself a brand new car and had indulged in a total of four short holiday breaks. Chantal was no longer someone working all hours and feeling that she had no money. Clearing her clutter changed her life.

People often ask me as a Feng Shui consultant, 'What is the one thing that I can do to get more money?'

Without question, I advise them: 'Go home and start clearing your clutter. Make way for some new energy to enter your life.'

My book, *Creating Space for Miracles*, covers this subject in much more depth, but let's start with the basics:

- What is clutter?
- What is your clutter?
- When are you going to clear it?

What Is Clutter?

The Feng Shui Academy definition of clutter is: anything that is not loved, not useful or not kept in an orderly manner.

If it helps, keep this definition posted up somewhere in your home until you have cleared all your clutter.

What Is Your Clutter?

You know, better than anyone else, where the clutter is in your home. What is your worst clutter? Is it the collection of unread magazines, the unworn clothes in the wardrobe or the stack of unwanted presents? Where does everything get hidden when you don't know what to do with it? Is it the garage, the loft or the spare bedroom that needs clearing? If your bedroom is cluttered, make it a priority area to be cleared. It will be giving your mind all the wrong messages as you fall asleep, and make you more likely to wake up feeling exhausted.

Maybe your home is free of physical clutter. To the external eye, it is clutter-free. How about your handbag or briefcase? How is the state of your car? What about your email inbox?

When Are You Going to Clear It?

Well done for facing up to the clutter in your home. The next step, of course, is to set about clearing it. When are you planning to be free of clutter? Where and when will you start? What will you need in order to clear the clutter? Bin bags, a skip, a helping hand, the 'drop off' times of your local charity shops, access to www.freecycle.org (a fabulous resource that transforms one person's clutter into another's riches). Make a list of what you'll need, and then mark the date in your calendar and commit to it, now!

Make way for wealth, commit to clearing your clutter now!

Exercise

'I commit to clear my clutter now.'

Identify what clutter is be cleared:

....

....

....
....
....
....

Identify what is required to clear it:

....
....
....
....
....
....

Sign and date the following statement: 'I commit to clearing my identified clutter on ....

Signature: ....

Witness Signature: ....

■ Case Study: Clutter Affects Your Health as Well as Your Wealth

The entrance hall was blocked with a pile of shoes. The kitchen entrance was blocked with a dishwasher, clearly on its way to being installed. The staircase was blocked with bin bags of items waiting to be cleared, and she physically couldn't get into her bedroom.

The owner of this house had been suffering with ill-health for a long time and she was in fear of losing her job. She was scheduled to have an operation on her bowels; shortly afterwards she was indeed made redundant.

Don't let your clutter overtake you. Start clearing it now!

If the clutter in your home is similar to the scene described above, please decide to get some help, now.

Living in a seriously cluttered space will sap you of energy. It becomes a 'chicken and egg' scenario, where you no longer have the energy to clear the clutter while the clutter continues to drain you of any energy that you do have.

On top of feeling constantly 'under the weather', your finances are likely to be suffering, too. In fact it is a shame that clutter-clearing services aren't funded by the Government, as they could have a huge positive impact on our communities.

Once you have made the decision to clear your clutter, you are more likely to find a way to get it cleared. Remember, clearing your clutter is a huge step forward to becoming a Money Magnet.

The good news is that almost as soon as you clear a space, the laws of nature dictate that it will be filled. If you combine your clutter-clearing with an intention to attract wealth, the 'void' is more likely to be filled with the energy of money.

■ *Case Study: Immediate Results*

You couldn't see the carpet in James' flat. A former electronics engineer, his clutter included electronic items in various states of repair. James was now a self-employed hypnotherapist. He was very good at what he did, but he was struggling to find any paying customers. As the clutter got worse, the bills mounted and James was soon in serious debt. He needed to start clearing his clutter.

Finally, one bright day James decided to donate one of his largest electronic items to someone he knew would appreciate it. Putting it in his car, he even delivered it by hand. No sooner was he back in his flat when the phone rang, 'Thank you so much, James,' said the recipient of his gift. 'Listen, mate, did you say that you do hypnotherapy? My wife needs a course of treatments …'

It was the first paying customer for James in months. Well done, James!

Clutter in Your Business

The same rules apply: if you have cluttered up your business with too much office clutter, too many products and too many people, it needs clearing. Looking at what's happening in these times of 'credit crunch' and mass redundancies, it is tempting to describe it as one massive clutter-clearing exercise. We all have to shed the unnecessary clutter in our lives to make way for progress and to create wealth.

■ *Case Study: Corporate Clutter-Clearing Boosts Profits*

When Dawn Gibbins MBE, former chairman of Flowcrete Group plc, learned about Feng Shui, the first thing that she did was to clear the clutter in her office headquarters. She then went on to clear up the diverse branding of many of her worldwide offices, and to streamline the product range.

In fewer than three years, turnover doubled. Last year Dawn sold her company for a sum reported to be £35 million. Watch out for Dawn's forthcoming book, *The Corporate Detox*.

Clearing Your Mind

It's not just clutter in your physical environment that is keeping you from attracting more money. It is clutter in the way you live your life and how you think. Let's look at where we can clear some space for more money by completing the following exercise.

The following are areas in your life that may have become cluttered and which may now be consuming too much of your energy. Take a look at the list and tick any that apply to you.

- Time-consuming friendships that you no longer value

- Unnecessarily long telephone calls

- TV – you know which programmes we're talking about here!

- Everyday tasks that you take on when you could choose not to

- Never-ending 'to do' lists

- Magazines and books that need to be read – or do they?

- Emails that need to be answered, or not, as the case may be

- Subscription email newsletters that you haven't the time to read

- Social or work commitments that no longer lift your spirits

- Concerns about never being 'good enough'

- Out-of-date grudges, guilt, blame or any negative emotion

- Gossip

- Thinking about all the clutter that needs sorting!

Now, for each one that you have ticked, write out underneath at least one alternative way of being. For example, if you find it hard to get off the phone with a friend, schedule in a meeting for just after your scheduled call time. If you feel guilty about something, decide to forgive yourself. If you are wasting energy blaming somebody, look instead for the positives in that person. If you don't wish to spend your time cleaning, think of alternative ways that the cleaning can get done. My nail technician, Karen, attracts extra income by renting out her spare rooms to international students. When I asked her about the extra cleaning and cooking involved, she told me how she has an arrangement with her grown-up daughter. Instead of paying rent, her daughter is responsible for these tasks. Karen has found an alternative way to get her household chores done. This means that she can spend more time with her fee-paying clients, doing what she loves to do and attracting more money into her bank account!

Like Karen, practise thinking outside the box to come up with ways to maximise the time you have available to be a Money Magnet.

■ *Case Study: Clearing Out the Christmas Card List*

Ann was an avid fan of the Christmas card list. Her lists went back more than 40 years, and included everyone who had ever sent her a Christmas card and everyone who had ever received her Christmas cards. Every year Ann posted out her cards religiously … until the year that her husband died.

That year she found out who her real friends were. They were the friends who noticed they hadn't had a Christmas card from her and who rang to check that she was OK.

The next year, Ann's Christmas card list was considerably shorter.

If you ticked 'TV', make a note of how many hours you spend watching television, then select what you now choose to watch. Make it a conscious choice. We covered earlier how our minds interpret what they see. Many programmes today are littered with bad news, poverty and violence. Are stories like this really going to help you to become a Money Magnet?

Unless you have already gained mastery over your thoughts in a way that can resist such messages, I suggest that you seriously limit your intake of television. Instead, choose to do something that lifts your spirits, whether that be reading a book or taking up dancing.

Focus Clears Mental Clutter

The easiest way to clear your mental clutter is to go back to the basics of 'What do I really want?' and 'What makes me feel happy?'

When you focus on what is important to you, you can clear the clutter that is getting in your way. If your 'to do' list is full of items that bore you or that seem more like daily chores, then you will find yourself going round in circles, never making any progress towards your goals.

Beware of daily priorities that include doing the household shopping and vacuuming the landing! These tasks will get done if they need to be done.

Your focus needs to link directly to your goals. For example, if your goal is to attract £100,000 into your bank account by the end of the year, your daily priorities will include at least one item that supports that goal, whether it be studying for a new qualification or telephoning a new prospect.

If you are not sure what you really want, don't worry! We'll be taking a closer look at that in the next chapter. In the meantime you may wish to look at your daily activities and make a list of what you don't want to do any more! By writing it down, you will be one step closer to clearing this type of clutter from your life – and anything that doesn't make you happy can be termed clutter.

Exercise: The Daily Time Audit

Note down in a diary for a week how you spend your time each day. At the end of the week, categorise the different activities under column headings such as: Fitness, Work, Household, Finance, Friends, Intimacy ... You can choose your own headings.

Are your activities evenly balanced across all columns? Is any activity consuming too much of your time? Would it be beneficial to reduce the time spent on this activity? Where would you reallocate the extra time you now have?

Resolve to make the necessary changes now.

Clear 'To Do' Lists

Nearly everyone I know uses 'to do' lists. Unfortunately, they often only succeed in making you feel exhausted. If you are going to bed with a picture in your mind of that never-ending list of things to do, you won't have the energy to do what you really want to do.

Instead, write down all the things that need doing as they come into your head during the day. Let's clear some space in your head for more important things, such as the inspiration that may lead you to attracting more money!

At the end of each day, find your list and decide on the top three things that need doing the next day. By choosing only three items, you will become better and better at prioritising and you will start clearing the clutter that's been holding you back. Remember, your daily priorities are those items that will move you forward or that will attract money, if that is one of your goals.

■ *Case Study: Being Busy Is Not Necessarily the Answer!*

After about six months of being self-employed, Jane wondered why she wasn't making more money. She was always busy. In fact, her friends often complained that she never had time to see them any more.

It wasn't until Jane did an audit of how she was spending her time that she realised what the problem was. Many of her activities involved doing what she'd always done, rather than looking at ways to move forward by doing something different.

When Jane created space in her diary for a brief holiday, she came back with lots of new money-making ideas for her business. She resolved to do at least one thing a day that she'd never done before.

As Jane became much better at prioritising items that would drive her business forward, her sales doubled and she found space in her diary to see her friends.

Keep Your Focus

When your focus is to attract more money, you have a yardstick by which to judge where you choose to place your effort. For example, given the choice between spending time writing this book and having a telephone chat with a friend, the book becomes my priority. I will schedule the chat with a friend as a reward once this chapter is completed. Similarly, if you earn more money per hour than you would pay a cleaner, you may choose to hire a cleaner!

The next couple of chapters expand on this subject as we elaborate on why it is important to follow your passion and to prioritise what is important to you, and why taking action is the fastest way to cut through any clutter and become a Money Magnet!

Checklist

- Do you hang on to junk mail for weeks?
- Is your bathroom full of products that you don't use?
- Do you have enough room for all of your books?
- Do you have a noticeboard that is layers deep in paper?
- Are your cupboards full of old medicines?
- Do you have useful gadgets that you never use?
- Or exercise equipment that you keep meaning to use?
- Is your car boot full of things that you might need one day?
- Do you have half-finished projects scattered around your home?
- Do you keep things that you never use because one day you might?

The money is already there.
The only thing preventing you from being rich is you.

8

Following Your Passion

'Give me a man who sings at his work.'
– Thomas Carlyle

Following your passion is the master route to becoming a Money Magnet. Anything less than this and the money manifested is likely to be temporary. Congratulations on reaching this part of the book and reaching this point in your life.

You can attract money by setting an intention, by performing a ceremony and by doing something different from your normal routine. You can start expecting to be rich and you can change your language and behaviours accordingly, but until you clear the clutter that's keeping you from your heart's desires, any money you attract will be just that, money. And as money is energy, it can disappear as soon it arrives, unless you uncover your own stream of abundance.

We have determined that money is received in exchange for value. Finding your gifts to the world and the best way to add real value is the secret to feeling truly fulfilled and wealthy in every sense. When you lift yourself towards your highest potential, you can become a Money Magnet. Funnily enough, the money arrives almost as an afterthought, as you become driven less by money and more by passion.

Money is worthless in itself. Someone stranded on a remote island for the rest of her life would be silly to wish to be a Money Magnet in those circumstances. Money flows to us when we are in our flow. We receive rewards for living at our highest possible potential, whatever that may be. A desire for money can distract us from our true passion, but it can also inspire us to lift our game in life and be all that we were born to be.

How do you find your passion? How do you find your flow?

The answer to finding your flow is to follow what makes you happy.

'Well,' I hear you ask. 'If it's that easy, why aren't we all richer?'

The answer is that most of us think we are doing what we want to do, but we are actually just playing it safe. It is a basic human need to want to be safe. We learned at a young age how to keep our main provider happy. Mummy was happy when we did what she wanted us to do. With our basic needs at stake, we learned how to please others from very early on and, in time, those other voices became so many that they drowned out the sound of our own personal and authentic voice. It is not surprising in this context that many people lose sight of their own identity.

Fortunately, this way of living is difficult and exhausting to sustain and so, sooner or later, many of us will experience what I refer to as a mid-life wake-up call. This is the moment when you catch a glimpse of your true self and from which there is no turning back.

The Mid-life Wake-up Call

How many people do you know who have ended up in a career because someone else, somewhere along the line, recommended it as the ideal route for them to take? It may have been a parent, a guardian, a peer or a teacher. They took the recommended option, only to 'wake up' mid-life and realise that it wasn't what they would have chosen for themselves. They are the lucky ones. Some people persevere in a job and live a life full of regret. Remember, you can't take the money with you.

Recently I was coaching Rachael, a woman in her sixties who had just 'woken up'. She remembered going to a public phone box at the age of 15 to make a call to a local rock band looking for a lead singer. She never made that call. When we explored her true desires, being a professional singer was still top of her list. The only difference was that now she was learning to trust herself and to honour her heart's desires. She knew that it might not always be plain sailing up ahead, but turning her back on herself again was no longer an option for her. Rachael is finally focusing on what truly makes her happy.

■ *Case Study: Follow Your Passion*

Claire followed her father into a career in accountancy. Then she realised that being an accountant didn't make her happy. She decided to follow her heart. She left accountancy and spent years training to be a naturopath, not necessarily knowing where that would take her but enjoying the thrill of doing something that made her happy.

Again, following her heart, Claire went on to set up www.lovelula.com, an online organic and natural beauty product shop. No doubt the attention to detail required in accountancy helped Claire create her website.

Claire is now in her flow and, as a result, Love Lula attracts millions of online visitors per month and is achieving impressive sales. There is no denying that Claire has worked hard for her success. It's amazing how committed you will be to a task when you are fuelled by passion!

- Do you know what truly makes you happy?
- When was the last time you felt joy or passion?
- What makes you leap out of bed in the morning?
- What are the events you are always on time for? (Lateness, no matter what the excuse, is a sign of your reluctance to be there.)
- What is it that you think you want to do?
- Is your heart really in what you do or want to do?

Finding out what really makes us happy can be challenging. One of the ways to get clearer on what you want is to start by looking at what you *don't* want.

Make a list of all the things currently in your life that you don't want: a boss you don't like, large household bills, a relationship that is going nowhere. It is important that you now rewrite your list, but this time reframe each item into a positive statement of what you *do* want: a great boss, enough money to do whatever you'd like to do, a committed loving relationship.

Exercise: Finding Out What You Want – By Looking at What You *Don't* Want!

Write down the things currently in your life that you don't want:

....

....

....

....

....

....

....

....

Now rewrite this list, reframing each one into a positive statement of what you *do* want. As you write out each new positive statement, cross out the item above that you didn't want.

....
....
....
....
....
....
....

■ *Case Study: Changing Direction*

It took a long time before Sue realised that she hated 'sales'. During that time she had had a number of different sales and sales manager posts. She was very earnest and hardworking. And she made a lot of 'noise' to cover the fact that she wasn't actually achieving the sales targets. Despite this, Sue even contemplated setting up her own company to advise people on selling!

Sue stayed in sales because she had always been in sales. Her CV was tailored to a sales career. Her identity was that of a salesperson.

When Sue acknowledged the truth, she felt an immense sense of freedom. She could now do whatever she wanted to do. Last time I spoke to Sue, she was living in Sydney, Australia and was very excited about setting up a new franchise venture called Positive Puppies. Sue is honouring her truth and her passion, and I have no doubt that it will make her a very wealthy woman, in a way that her sales career never did. Well done, Sue.

Forget the Money and Focus on Your Passion

You are reading a book entitled *How to Become a Money Magnet!* and I am telling you to forget the money! Yes, that's right. By all means set an intention of how much money you wish to manifest, and take responsibility for how much money you currently have. Follow all the steps in this book so far. And then be prepared to let go of your financial dream and to trust that when you follow your passion, it will happen.

Miracles happen when you follow your passion!

Miracle Club

Two years ago I received the inspiration for Miracle Club. It was to be a worldwide network of people supporting each other to achieve their full potential. Combining the principle of the Law of Attraction with the practice of group coaching sessions, it would create a haven of positive thought. It was a brilliant vision and I told everyone I knew about Miracle Club.

I registered the company and I bought the domain name www.miracleclub.com, and then I was advised to do a business plan to work out how it was going to earn me some money. Nothing happened. I never seemed to have the time or the confidence to get round to doing this business plan. I was distracted by so many other things and by what everyone else around me was doing.

One day I finally realised that I really was the happiest I could ever be when I was inspiring others to believe in themselves and in their dreams. Whenever one of my students told me another story of his or her success, my heart seemed to explode with joy. So instead of asking, 'How can I earn money from this?' I asked myself a different question: 'How can I make a real difference using my skill and passion?'

> Instead of asking yourself, 'How can I earn money from this?' ask, 'How can I make a real difference using my skill and passion?'

I realised that the people who needed Miracle Club the most were those with the least money to pay for it. I wanted to reach the people who had given up on their dreams, who had lost their jobs and who had no money. Once I was clear on what I really wanted, I set an intention to attract funding for Miracle Club. Within a week, I found a sponsor to fund places on Miracle Club ... and Miracle Club was officially born!

Now is the time to find your passion and to let it explode into a gift for the rest of humanity. You were not born to play small or to live a boring life. You have a natural desire to be happy and to grow into your full potential. Now is the time to wake up and start getting excited about every single day of your life!

> *Imagine ...*
>
> Imagine if the acorn 'couldn't be bothered' to grow into a magnificent oak tree.
>
> Imagine if the swallow listened to the budgie in its cage and decided not to migrate this year?
>
> Imagine if the caterpillar 'had better things to do' than to go through a period of transition to become a butterfly?
>
> Honour yourself and do what makes you happy and you will grow into all you can be.

Finding Your Heart's Desire

'It is the heart always that sees, before the head can see.' – Thomas Carlyle

Finding out what you really want can be quite challenging if you haven't done it for a while. The following exercise is based on one described by Jack Canfield in his book *The Power of Focus*.

Exercise: Finding Your Immediate Heart's Desire

Write out a list of 101 things that you want to be, do or have. Start with 40 things. Then add another 30, and then a final 30. Add a last item just to tip you over the 100 mark.

The first 40 items may be relatively easy to think up but the secret to success in this exercise is to reach at least 101 items.

Only once you have your full list, select all the short-term items that you would like within the next year. Rewrite them onto a separate list, and write this new list on the far left-hand side of a blank piece of paper. Now in true 'knock-out tournament' style, take two items at a time and, as fast as you can, select the one that you want most. It is important to complete this exercise at great speed. If possible, compete with a friend to see who finishes first.

Your first answer is likely to be your heart's desire. If you take longer, it allows time for your brain to get engaged and the exercise won't work. Continue the process to the bottom of the list and then start again with the chosen options, and again until eventually you reach the top eight, four, two and eventually your top number one priority for right now.

Phew! Now you can relax! The rest will be so easy ...

What Is Your Top Priority?

I remember the first time I did this exercise. My list was full of impressive ideals, and yet my number one priority was to lose weight! I was hugely disappointed. 'How shallow,' I thought. Then I realised that if I were to take the necessary steps to slim down, it would mean that I would be showing more respect for myself. And yes, self-respect was a good number one for my list!

The second time I did this exercise I discovered a new desire: I wanted to have the chance to present a regular slot on radio where I could inspire others to think more positively and to take responsibility for their reality.

One of the main benefits of the 101 exercise is that it invites you to think outside of your normal comfort zone. The first 40, even 60, are likely to be familiar to you. When you complete the exercise to the full 101, or more, you may uncover heart's desires that you were previously unaware of.

Enjoy the freedom of exploration as you create your list. Follow your heart, not your head.

Don't think 'How?', think 'Wow!'

Smile while you write your list. Enjoy the indulgence of joy as you imagine the possibilities. This is a fun exercise. Have fun doing it!

Find Your Heart's Desire and the Money Will Come

When we are happy, our energy shifts to a higher vibration. We start to attract more things that make us happy. So it makes sense for you to find out what will make you the happiest ... and then start from there.

Katie came to me for Feng Shui coaching. She wanted to run her own interior design business – at least, that's what she told me when we first met. When we ran through her 101 list, her heart's desire turned out to be to own a camper van! Her face lit up with joy at the very mention of it.

> Once you get clear on what you really want, everything starts to fall into place. Attracting what you need, including money, becomes easy.

I asked Katie, 'What do you need to do next in order to own your own camper van?'

'Oh,' she said. 'I need to get a job.' (I told you this was simple!)

'And do you have any particular job in mind?' I asked.

'Oh, yes,' Katie said. 'I know of the perfect job that I can do. I just need to make one phone call and the job is mine.'

It was incredible. Katie already had the means to her end. She'd just been looking in the wrong direction! She hadn't paid full attention to her true heart's desire.

I enquired whether the job was something that she really wanted to do.

'Oh, yes,' she said again. 'It's with my favourite charity. I already donate money to them and it will be a real joy to spend my time getting other people to contribute to a cause that I believe in. I think I'll be really good at it!'

As there was commission to be earned, I have no doubt that Katie will manifest the money to buy her van within the timescale she has set herself.

The Challenge of Following Your Passion

First of all you need to be clear of clutter so that you can feel your heart's desire and know your true passion. We are often distracted by the expectations of others, or by 'just getting on with it'.

You have to be prepared that what was your passion at one time might now have shifted to something else, and that's completely OK.

You need to honour your passion by having the self-belief and focus to act upon it. Sometimes it is far less scary to fail at something when your heart just isn't in it, than when it is a passion that goes to the very core of your being.

In the next chapter we'll look at bringing together all the pieces of the puzzle in what I call the FAB process.

Checklist

- What was your childhood ambition?
- What did you love to do as a child?
- When do you feel most alive?
- When do you feel happiest?
- When do you feel most fulfilled?

- What makes you sad?
- What makes you angry or frustrated?
- What do you care passionately about?
- What are you very good at?
- What is your gift?
- What are you waiting for?

The money is already there.
The only thing preventing you from
being rich is you.

9

*Working with the
FAB Principle*

*'Conviction is worthless unless
it is converted into conduct.'*
– **Thomas Carlyle**

F-A-B stands for Focus, Action and Belief. In brief, you
want to *focus* on what is important to you, you want to
take *action* and you want to *believe* in yourself and your
goals. It is simple, really.

If you want to be a Money Magnet, you want to get into
the flow of what makes you feel happy and fulfilled. Or,
in my language, whatever gives you an incredible buzz!

■ Case Study: Richard Branson Acts on His Passion and Belief

At a very young age and to encourage the
development of his character, Richard was
dropped off a mile from home and left to find
his own way back. What an inspiring lesson in
encouraging self-belief. Unlike most of us, who

learned how to survive by keeping others happy, in that instance Richard learned that he could actually rely on his own judgement, independent of others.

Throughout an incredibly successful career, Richard has consistently followed his heart's desires, often in complete contrast to the wishes of his advisors and family. He demonstrates belief in himself and in his visions. He stays focused on the vision, and achieves it by literally taking one step at a time. He is driven more by passion than money, and yet Richard Branson is a perfect example of a Money Magnet.

For more about Richard Branson's inspiring life, take a look at his autobiography, *Losing My Virginity* (Virgin Books, 2007).

Once you've identified your heart's desire, you need to take some action. This may seem obvious, but I am regularly amazed by students who have read books on the Law of Attraction and who believe that they can become wealthy purely by the use of visualisation.

Visualisation *is* a very powerful tool. Just ask any athlete. When you expect to be rich and you feel what it would feel like to be rich, you will then start to attract opportunities to be rich. Effectively, you will have transformed yourself into an energetic Money Magnet.

Now, to make it real, you need to *act* on the opportunities presented to you. An athlete may visualise winning the Olympics, but unless she takes enough action to ensure she gets a place on the team, she can't win Olympic Gold no matter how much she has visualised standing on the podium.

Interestingly, the action you take is not always directly linked to the result. That doesn't matter. All you need to do is start taking steps towards your goal and the opportunities will present themselves.

What Are the First Steps You Could Take to Becoming a Money Magnet?

- Have you done an audit of your finances?

- Have you cleared your clutter?

- Did you ask for that promotion?

- Have you prepared your CV for that job?

- Have you made the phone call that needs making?

- Have you started that book that needs writing?

- Have you written your business plan?

- Can you get up an hour earlier just to start doing some of these things?

Our minds get cluttered up with irrelevant detail. We can go full days, even weeks, without making any progress towards our goals. Once you have found what is important to you, whether it is losing weight, starting a business, writing a book or saving 10 per cent of your earnings each month, keep a tight focus on it. Every morning, wake up and remind yourself what is most important to you. I often think about this in terms of having three key priorities. For example, my top three at the moment are:

1. Finish this book

2. Be 10 stone

3. Achieve £100,000.

So, a typical day at the moment will start with me writing. However, I build in an opportunity for exercise sometime in the day, usually with a friend. By the way, I would only ever choose to do exercise that makes me happy. My favourites at the moment are going for bike rides, brisk walking into town and belly dancing. The only other thing that I will allow to interrupt my writing will be anything that is related to maximising my income. Again, I am only referring to items that make me happy. These could be delivering a public talk, coaching a client or running a Miracle Club class.

Life is about balance. Some people may argue that one should focus on only one thing at a time until it's finished. Yes, I agree, as long as you allow some breaks in the process. Interrupting my writing to see a friend for a bike ride or to coach a client often provides me with just the inspiration that I need to continue.

When you start every day focused on specific goals, you have more chance of success and you create more free time for recreation. It is easier to say 'No' to activities that are not aligned to your goals, and to say 'Yes' to fun activities when you know that you have done your best towards your goal that day.

In the last chapter we looked at how important it is to uncover your passion and your gifts in order to become a true Money Magnet. We looked at how to find your heart's immediate desire, and some of you may have found that it isn't actually 'money' after all. Taking what you found to be the most important focus for you at this moment in time, commit to taking the steps needed to allow it to happen.

Exercise: Focused Action

State your top three immediate desires. Put a timescale on each one, such as 'I am to have £50,000 in my bank account in September' or 'I am going to be presenting on TV before the end of this year.'

Take a moment to FEEL what it is like to have achieved this goal.

Now, for each item, write down one thing that you are going to do today to attract this possibility. And do it.

Before you retire to bed this evening, take your three priorities again and write down another three immediate actions, one for each vision, for the following day. Only change the focus once your heart is happy that it has been achieved.

Taking action is the quickest way to clear the clutter that's stopping you from being all you can be.

Taking action is less about 'making it happen' and more about responding to life's opportunities. As in the earlier example, I couldn't make a success of Miracle Club until I responded from a point of desire and passion. My motivation to act had to come from the heart, not the head.

Life is not meant to be hard work. We can be disciplined and focused in our approach. We may suffer setbacks, but as long as we stay aligned to what truly makes us happy, we will be wealthy. Focused action that is driven by desire is powerful and can achieve miracles. Doing what we love to do and what we were born to do offers value to the world. In offering value and in honouring ourselves, we find true self-worth. Our self-worth is then reflected back to us in the value we attract and, in today's modern economy, this will lead us to become Money Magnets.

■ Case Study: Living Your Passion

Chantal Cooke is an excellent example of how we can live our passion.

Combining her love of radio with her passion for the environment, Chantal established the radio station Passion for the Planet. It's an innovative concept featuring world music and brief three-minute interviews on interesting and often alternative subjects. Chantal absolutely adores what she does. She is naturally good at it and is never short of people to interview!

Chantal is clear on her goals, and every day she follows a very focused and action-orientated agenda. Chantal lives her life to the full, maximising every single moment. Once Chantal had cleared her clutter, she became a natural Money Magnet.

Money, or lack of it, is the clue, rarely the destination. People have a passion but they don't push it.

> 'Let each become all that he was created capable of being.' – *Thomas Carlyle*

'So what about all the people you know who are following their passion and yet can't find two pennies to rub together?' I hear you ask, 'What about the struggling artist or writer, the massage therapist, the chef who dreams of owning his own restaurant? Where are they going wrong?'

They are stopping just short of their potential. They will go as far as the cliff edge but they may be afraid to jump off it. Their lack of money is the clue that there is more for them to do. In order for us all to reach our full potential, we have to be prepared to abandon our comfort zone.

> 'The turtle only makes progress when its neck is stuck out.' – *Rollo May*

By pushing yourself to do something challenging that may make you feel uncomfortable and even a little scared, you will bust through your comfort zone. As your comfort zone grows, so does your capacity for increased wealth. Don't settle for being comfortable when you have so much more to give to the world. Seize the challenge of being the best you can be and go for it!

The good news is that if you have found your passion and you are good at it, the FAB principle will ensure that you become a Money Magnet. Keep focused on your dream, start taking some positive action towards it and believe in yourself and your goals. One final tip: if you still have a nagging suspicion that you're just not good enough to aim so high, pretend for the moment that you are good enough, and do it anyway. Get used to busting through your redundant comfort zone!

It all comes down to value. Remember, money is about an exchange of value. If you truly value yourself and the service that you provide, you will project that sense of value in your aura. Do you truly think that you are worth more than you are currently receiving? Your thoughts are what have created your current reality. The good news is that if you have found your passion and you are good at it, you have the potential to become a Money Magnet. Follow the steps in the preceding chapters to change the pattern of your current thoughts.

Make an intention to become a Money Magnet. Mark the shift with a ceremony of some sort or by doing something radically different to your normal behaviour to mark the moment. Start to expect more money to come to you and change the way you talk about your situation. Use affirmations and visualisations to support your transition. And most of all, act now to clear your clutter! It could be the only thing that's left to stand in the way of your success.

■ Case Study: You Are the Only Obstacle to Your Success

Sharon became one of my clients after hearing me give a talk entitled 'I'm Following My Passion, Now Where's the Money?' Hearing me, she suddenly realised why she was struggling financially with her business.

'It's me,' she said to her friends. 'I'm the only thing standing in the way of my success. It's me!' Her friends looked on blankly. They didn't understand. 'Isn't it the economic climate or the lack of business funding that is at fault?'

Following her moment of clarity, Sharon booked in for three months of coaching. She cleared the pattern of 'poor me' that had plagued her since she was small. Sharon took responsibility for her thoughts and for her life to date. In doing so, she cleared the way to becoming a Money Magnet.

Almost immediately Sharon started attracting lucrative opportunities for her business.

Checklist

- What have you been meaning to get round to doing?

- What would you really like to do if only you had the time?

- What could you do once you have the money to do it?

- How can you start to do it right now?

- What would you like to do that maybe others don't want you to do?

- Is there a way you can start doing it now?

- What next steps are you scared of taking?

- What new habit are you choosing to adopt?

- What are you committed to doing this week?

- What are your three most pressing goals?

- What have you done to progress each one today?

*The money is already there.
The only thing preventing you from being rich is you.*

10

Once a Magnet,
Always a Magnet!

'When I chased after money, I never had enough.
When I got my life on purpose and focused on
giving of myself and everything that arrived into
my life, then I was prosperous.'

– Wayne Dyer

The science is proven. We are energetic beings and we attract what we think about. Your life is a reflection of your thoughts, both conscious and unconscious.

Change your thoughts and you change your life. Adopt some Money Magnet habits and you will become a Money Magnet for life.

You decided to become a Money Magnet when you committed to reading this book in its entirety. You make it happen when you apply the exercises and instructions in the book. If you want to increase the amount of money in your life, you want to start thinking differently and you want to start changing your habits.

The Habits and Thoughts of a Money Magnet!

- You love and respect yourself.

- You value what you offer in return for money.

- You respect money by knowing how much you have.

- You respect money by spending it wisely.

- You can talk about money easily and in an appropriate way.

- You sleep well at night knowing that you are financially secure.

- You have time for yourself.

- You enjoy what you do.

- You are happy most of the time.

- You share your happiness with others.

- You have a clear vision of what you desire in the future.

- You experience your vision daily.

- You look at inspiring images every day in your home and office.

- You make a clear intention when you want something.

- You celebrate the riches already in your life.

- You are naturally generous.

- You compliment others and receive compliments easily.

- You stay on top of your clutter: in your home, office, body and mind.

- You take responsibility, knowing that thoughts attract things to you.

- You maintain a daily focus on what is important to you.

- You take action on any inspiration received.

- You believe in yourself.

- You relax regularly to let go of all the mental clutter.

- You take regular holidays.

- You enjoy a healthy work/life balance.

You live in an abundant universe and you were born to live an abundant life. You are unique. You are powerful. It is time to celebrate the wonder of life and the wonder of you. It is time to look to your true self, and to cut through the cloud of limiting thoughts and low self-worth. Then you can be the magnificent magnet that you were born to be.

By finding your heart's desire, you can follow your path and let others benefit from the true value you have to give to the world. And in giving value, you will receive value. In feeling worthy, you will be blessed with worthy abundance.

Follow the Steps in This Book to Attract Money Regularly

- Understand how your thoughts dictate the quality of your life.

- Be clear and specific on how much money you wish to attract.

- Make friends with money and understand your current financial situation.

- Break your existing pattern towards money.

- Start expecting to receive more money.

- Become rich in your imagination, your language and your actions.

- Clear space for more money.

- Follow your passion and you will attract money.

- Act on all opportunities that come your way.

- Stay connected to your truth and you'll stay connected to abundance.

In Feng Shui the human being is the connection between heaven and earth. The heart is the connecting point within the human.

When we connect with our heart's desires, we tap into the unlimited abundance of the universe.

The tricky bit, of course, is staying connected!

Staying Connected to Abundance

It sounds easy to stay in touch with what we really want, but how many times have you gone along with the crowd, just for the sake of convenience? Maybe you'd love to leave your job but it feels scary to be without the regular pay packet? In order to stay connected, you have to start honouring your own desires. Listen to your truth, listen to what you really want, and then take just one action towards achieving it right now. Look for the one action that feels the most uncomfortable and scary. When you take that one action towards your dreams, you will feel a huge sense of relief. You will know that you are on track. Avoid the scary step outside of your comfort zone and you risk going round in the same circle forever.

The trap is when you look at what you currently have rather than what you wish to have. You stay in the same job in order to have money. If you are miserable in the job, your thoughts will not be the kind to attract money. Like Jo earlier in this book, you are likely to attract redundancy or ill-health. Sickness is often a sign from your body that you are ignoring yourself.

■ *Case Study: Ill-health Is Your Body Shouting at You!*

Debbie arrived at the class out of breath and overweight. She told us how her job was making her ill. She was working too many hours, because 'it won't get done if I don't do it.' She told us how she'd love to leave her job but they couldn't afford to have one less salary in the family. In fact she didn't dare tell her husband that she didn't want to do the job any more.

Can you see now where Debbie was going wrong? Debbie had been ignoring her heart's desires for so long that her body was now 'shouting' at her to stop doing something that she hated. Shortly afterwards Debbie was signed off on sick leave.

Fortunately Debbie had taken the first step by coming to the class. Once she acknowledged that she was blocking her own path to health, wealth and happiness, Debbie then found the courage to tell her husband. To her surprise he was 100 per cent supportive of her desire to leave work. He wanted a happy and healthy wife.

Debbie used the classes to find out what she really wanted to do. She rediscovered her love of writing and has already taken action, putting pen to paper to write her first screenplay. The last I heard Debbie was leaving work with a £50,000 leaving package.

Do What You Say You Are Going to Do

By honouring your truth, you honour yourself. By doing what you say you are going to do, you start to trust your own word. You start to trust yourself. You get more and more in touch with what you want and you start to trust that your heart's desires are OK, irrespective of what others may be thinking. In honouring your own word, you effectively give yourself a massive dose of self-esteem.

Now you are radiating like those who truly respect themselves. Consciously or unconsciously, people will be drawn to you for your magnetic self-confidence. You will attract opportunities from people of integrity. Now that you truly value yourself, others will value you, and you naturally become a Money Magnet.

Stay Grateful

A while ago I was introduced to the HeartMath© system. It monitors the electromagnetic rhythms of your heart. Fascinated, I allowed myself to be hooked up to the monitor and I watched as the screen showed a very erratic pulsing line. 'Now relax,' I was told, 'and we'll see if we can slow down your energies to achieve a more relaxed pulse.' I relaxed ... and nothing happened. My heart energies still appeared 'all over the place' despite my relaxed state. 'Try being grateful' came the suggestion.

Understanding how important it is to be connected to our hearts, I was eager to be able to calm mine down. As soon as I started to think 'grateful thoughts', I watched as the line on the screen reached a steady pulse. It was incredible.

It made sense of all the teachings that I'd read about: gratitude has incredible power.

> Gratitude is the key to attracting our heart's wishes. If you are feeling grateful you will attract more things for which to be grateful.

Writing down what makes you feel grateful is an excellent idea. I can strongly recommend the exercise of writing a minimum of five things in a special 'gratitude' journal each night before you go to sleep. Just imagine how your mind will get to work on attracting more for you while you sleep! It is a lovely way to end any day.

Exercise

Write down some things that you are grateful for in your life right now.

....

....

....

....

....

....

....

Be Happy!

Being happy is a decision. In every moment of the day, you can choose to be happy. When you choose to be happy, you will feel good and you will attract good things. It makes sense. So why are we all so miserable? It is only a habit. It's now time to break that habit.

Exercise: Get Happy!

Practise smiling, at least eight times a day.

Say 'hello' to strangers, with a smile.

Look for something beautiful and smile when you discover it.

Keep your head up high.

Keep a gratitude journal.

Complete your top three priorities each day.

Take time out to play.

Be silly.

Do something that makes someone else happy.

Do something that you've always wanted to do.

Remember a moment when you were filled with joy.

Find something that makes you laugh.

Be with happy people.

Mix with Other Money Magnets!

It is important to surround yourself with other like-minded people. Do you know that you are the energetic equivalent of the five people you spend most of your time with? What do the people around you say about you? Do they lift your spirits when they enter the room? Can they easily see the positive in most situations? Are they following their heart's desires and living lives packed with passion?

Look out for networks or meetings of like-minded people.

Mirror Magnets

If you have people in your life who are always moaning or who feel that they have been treated badly, whatever you do, do not try to change them. By all means, leave a helpful book lying around for them to read, but certainly don't expect them to read it! These people are extremely helpful to you in your quest to become a Money Magnet!

Energetically they are there as a reflection of the parts of you that you have not yet acknowledged. When you are working on changing your thoughts to become a Money Magnet, this can be really helpful.

Remember, 'Like attracts like' and there is no exception. Once you acknowledge where you are still moaning, or where you feel that you have been treated badly, the energies will change. When you shift to a more positive energy, one of three things is likely to happen regarding the negative person in your life:

1. Either the other person will change his behaviour, or

2. He will move away from you, or

3. You will simply no longer be affected by that aspect of the person.

When you are surrounded by positive, happy, wealthy people, you will know that you are on the right track.

If you still have a few 'needy' or 'stingy' friends, look to see where you are 'needy' or 'stingy' yourself. Don't just ditch these friends, as you will only attract more of the same kind until you acknowledge those parts of you.

Value Yourself and You Will Attract Value

The more you love yourself, the more you will have to give to others. The more you value yourself, the more value you will have to offer others.

- Do you value your gifts?

- Do you appreciate all your strengths?

- What is it that you can offer to others that will make a difference?

- What is it that makes you really happy?

- Do it.

Decide now to start valuing yourself more. You are a precious commodity and worthy of being looked after. What do you need to perform at your highest? What drives you? Take some time to really get to know yourself.

Exercise: Finding Your True Value

Make a list of your strengths and skills. Ask a friend if you need to.

Include all your qualifications and achievements to date, and anything good that anyone has ever said about you.

....
....
....
....
....
....
....
....
....
....
....
....
....
....
....
....
....

Ability to Receive

<u>Exercise: Get Ready to Receive</u>

- Are you really ready to receive lots of money?

- Are you ready to give your gifts to the world and to receive your true worth?

- Do you have a sneaky idea of exactly what you need to do next in your life in order to attract more money? If so, write it down NOW.

How Good Are You at Receiving?

Can you remember how you responded the last time someone paid you a compliment? I've overheard so many people reject the positive vibration being sent their way. For example, 'Oh, I love the dress you're wearing.' 'Oh, this old thing. It was only a few pounds in the sale two summers ago.'

Or 'Congratulations on your new job. What an achievement!' 'Oh, it was nothing really ... just in the right place at the right time, I guess.'

Next time the person paying the compliment might just not bother. After all, the 'knock-back' of the compliment is effectively down-valuing their point of view. How silly of them to have thought it was a lovely dress when it was only a two-year-old sale bargain? How stupid was it to imply that you have done well when the job was always 'in the bag'?

> *'What if you gave someone a gift, and they neglected to thank you for it – would you be likely to give them another? Life is the same way. In order to attract more of the blessings that life has to offer, you must truly appreciate what you already have.'*
> – Ralph Marston

When the money comes knocking on your door, are you ready to receive it as graciously as you would a compliment? When the inspiration for a new business idea comes into your head, are you ready to accept it or are you thinking 'That's a great idea – for someone else.'

> The correct response to a compliment is to say 'Thank you.'
>
> The correct response to an inspiration is to act on it.

You are offered plenty of opportunities to attract more money into your life. You just need to turn around, open your eyes, stretch out your arms and say, 'Thank you!'

Now might be a good time to start practising the art of receiving. Why not experiment with the following exercise in your own time?

Compliment Exercise

Over the next week, start paying people compliments and listen to their responses.

How do you feel?

Listen out for compliments directed at yourself (often we don't even hear them!).

When you receive a compliment yourself, practise receiving it graciously with a simple 'Thank you'. For this week only, resist the temptation to return the compliment immediately.

Practise receiving and allow the 'gift' to settle. A quick retort to a compliment is a bit like spending all your wages as soon as you get them. Allow some time for appreciation.

It may also be worth asking yourself, 'How often do I accept or request help with my life, my home, my business?' Many of us try to do it all ourselves. To become a Money Magnet, you need to let go a little so that you can start to receive more openly.

Letting Go

Letting go of wanting to become a Money Magnet is all part of the process. You can let go when you know that you already are a Money Magnet!

You attract whatever you think about. You now think that you are worth so much more than when you first picked up this book. You know your true value and you value yourself. You have an inner knowing that is about to manifest in your outer world. Keep that faith and let go of being a 'wannabe' ...

Congratulations! You Are a Money Magnet!

Each person has their own journey. The steps outlined in this book have worked for hundreds of my students, and I have witnessed some amazing financial breakthroughs as a result of the 'How to Become a Money Magnet!' workshop.

Once you set an intention, you set in motion the attraction of that possibility. You are then likely to attract people and opportunities to support you in reaching your desired reality. Follow your intuition and explore every opportunity that comes your way. It could be a business opportunity, a friend's advice or a particular therapy.

Sometimes it is difficult to point to the one thing that made you a Money Magnet. More often it will involve a number of steps and points of clarity along a winding road, before you emerge triumphant.

The money is already there. The only thing preventing you from being rich is you.

■ *Case Study: Helen's Story*

'From a young age, I remember my mum and grandmother saying to me, "We never win anything in this family." That sentence stayed with me throughout my childhood and through many of my adult years. I did not question it, as I thought that was my destiny.

'All that changed when I began my coaching journey in 2005. I became exposed to new and more inspiring ways of thinking. All of a sudden I became fed up of settling for second best and I decided to make a conscious intention to become more successful, like many of the people I had read about. I started using intentions to find car parking spaces and – lo and behold – whenever I'd go into a car park, there would be a space waiting for me. Then a few days later, I saw a competition in a magazine to win £1,000 of Marks and Spencer vouchers. All it required was to complete a slogan. I sent it off. Then I got a message back saying that I'd won!

'Being encouraged by this, I then decided to focus on what I really wanted. I was at a charity lunch and one of the prizes there was a beautiful £300 watch. Before the lunch started I was looking at the prizes and imagining myself wearing it. When my name got picked out of the hat, I felt as though I had fulfilled my goal.

'Two other great wins have happened since then – a £25,000 package at Stockport County Football Club for the 2007-08 season (which they finished with a promotion) and a course of singing lessons with celebrated singing coach David Gregory.

'When I think about how all these things have happened, I would say that the way I achieved them was first to focus on them and then to take action. The focusing is the lever that makes you take the action to win.'

– Helen Adams

Recommended Reading and Resources

Why not write in and tell us how you transformed into a Money Magnet? The more stories we collect, the more we can inspire others to step up and be all they can be. Remember, your destiny is to be rich. Enjoy it!

Your stories can be emailed to mc@marieclairecarlyle. com with the subject header 'I am a Money Magnet!'

Alternatively you might want to send us a letter. Send it to:

'I am a Money Magnet!'
Netherwood House
Whitchurch Road
Chester CH3 6AF.

Remember to include your contact details so that we can reach you, should we decide to publish your story.

If you are interested in attending the one-day How to Become a Money Magnet workshop, in becoming a Money Magnet coach or receiving one-to-one Money Magnet coaching, please register your interest at www.marieclairecarlyle.com or email us directly at mc@marieclairecarlyle.com. If you are interested in joining the Miracle Club and benefiting from affordable group coaching, please join us at www. miracleclub.com.

Thank you – *Marie-Claire*

Further Reading

Duncan Bannatyne, *Anyone Can Do It* (Orion, 2006)

Sir Richard Branson, *Losing My Virginity* (Virgin Books, 2007)

Jack Canfield, *The Power of Focus* (HCi, 2000)

Diana Cooper, *Transform Your Life* (2nd revised edn; Piatkus, 1998)

------, *A Little Light on the Spiritual Laws* (Mobius, 2000)

Noel Edmonds, *Positively Happy* (Vermilion, 2007)

Lynn Grabhorn, *Excuse Me, Your Life Is Waiting* (Mobius, 2005)

Napoleon Hill, *Think and Grow Rich* (deluxe edn; Capstone, 2009)

Susan Jeffers, *Feel the Fear and Do It Anyway* (20th anniversary edn; Vermilion, 2007)

Paul McKenna, *I Can Make You Rich* (Bantam, 2008)

Lynne McTaggart, *The Field* (Element, 2003)

Barbel Mohr, *Cosmic Ordering for Beginners* (Hay House, 2006)

Michael Neill, *You Can Have What You Want* (Hay House, 2009)

James Redfield, *The Celestine Prophecy* (Bantam, 1994)

Joe Vitale, *The Attractor Factor* (John Wiley & Sons, 2005)

Nick Williams, *The Work We Were Born to Do* (Element, 2000)

Hay House Titles of Related Interest

Ask and It Is Given,
by Esther and Jerry Hicks

Just Get On With It,
by Ali Campbell

Cosmic Ordering for Beginners,
by Barbel Mohr

Dowsing,
by Elizabeth Brown

Inspired Destiny,
by Dr John Demartini

Happiness in Hard Times,
by Andrew Matthews

You Can Have What You Want,
by Michael Neill

We hope you enjoyed this Hay House book.
If you would like to receive a free catalogue featuring additional
Hay House books and products, or if you would like information
about the Hay Foundation, please contact:

Hay House UK Ltd
292B Kensal Road • London W10 5BE
Tel: (44) 20 8962 1230; Fax: (44) 20 8962 1239
www.hayhouse.co.uk

***

Published and distributed in the United States of America by:
Hay House, Inc. • PO Box 5100 • Carlsbad, CA 92018-5100
Tel: (1) 760 431 7695 or (1) 800 654 5126;
Fax: (1) 760 431 6948 or (1) 800 650 5115
www.hayhouse.com

***

Published and distributed in Australia by:
Hay House Australia Ltd • 18/36 Ralph Street • Alexandria, NSW 2015
Tel: (61) 2 9669 4299, Fax: (61) 2 9669 4144
www.hayhouse.com.au

***

Published and distributed in the Republic of South Africa by:
Hay House SA (Pty) Ltd • PO Box 990 • Witkoppen 2068
Tel/Fax: (27) 11 467 8904
www.hayhouse.co.za

***

Published and distributed in India by:
Hay House Publishers India • Muskaan Complex • Plot No.3
B-2• Vasant Kunj • New Delhi - 110 070
Tel: (91) 11 41761620; Fax: (91) 11 41761630
www.hayhouse.co.in

***

Distributed in Canada by:
Raincoast • 9050 Shaughnessy St • Vancouver, BC V6P 6E5
Tel: (1) 604 323 7100
Fax: (1) 604 323 2600

***

Sign up via the Hay House UK website to receive the Hay House
online newsletter and stay informed about what's going on with your
favourite authors. You'll receive bimonthly announcements
about discounts and offers, special events, product highlights,
free excerpts, giveaways, and more!
www.hayhouse.co.uk

JOIN THE HAY HOUSE FAMILY

As the leading self-help, mind, body and spirit publisher in the UK, we'd like to welcome you to our family so that you can enjoy all the benefits our website has to offer.

EXTRACTS from a selection of your favourite author titles

COMPETITIONS, PRIZES & SPECIAL OFFERS Win extracts, money off, downloads and so much more

LISTEN to a range of radio interviews and our latest audio publications

CELEBRATE YOUR BIRTHDAY An inspiring gift will be sent your way

LATEST NEWS Keep up with the latest news from and about our authors

ATTEND OUR AUTHOR EVENTS Be the first to hear about our author events

iPHONE APPS Download your favourite app for your iPhone

HAY HOUSE INFORMATION Ask us anything, all enquiries answered

join us online at **www.hayhouse.co.uk**

292B Kensal Road, London W10 5BE
T: 020 8962 1230 E: info@hayhouse.co.uk